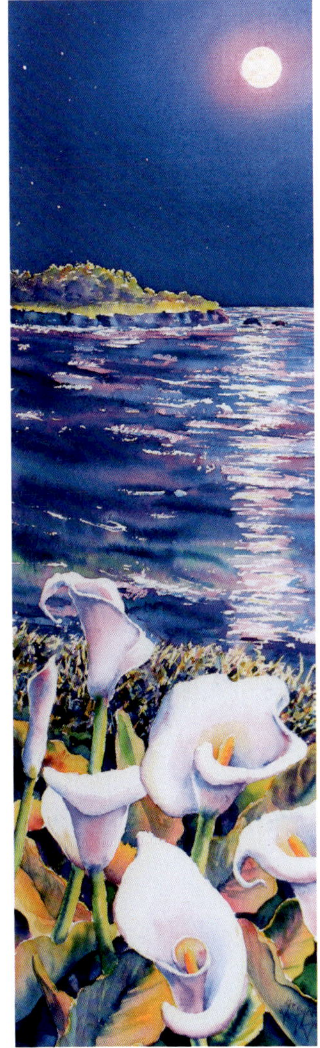
Coast Lilies, watercolor

MENDOCINO

PAINTINGS BY **DAVID GREGORY**

WORDS BY **JOHN BEAR**

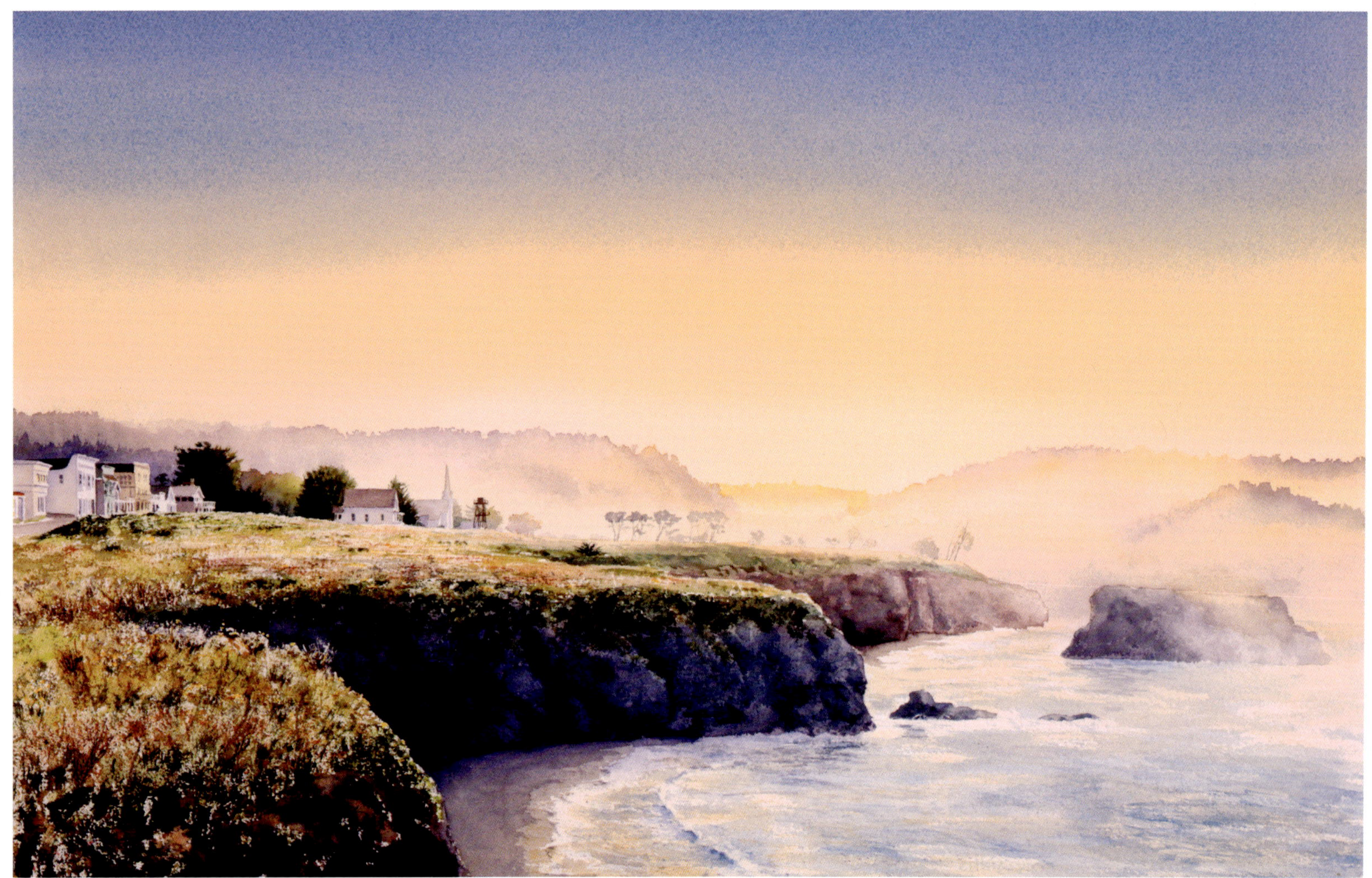

Headlands Morning, watercolor

People keep trying to put their finger on what it is that makes Mendocino so special. After all, there are thousands of other rural towns of comparable size and isolation, but few, if any, with the same mystique, the same kind of reputation, the same kind of magic. One good answer was supplied by a Midwestern tourist, who noted that "Mendocino is one of the very few places in the world where the locals and tourists do the same things for pleasure."

David

For Renée
whose love, unwavering support,
optimism, and humor constantly
inspire me.

John

For Marina
with love and grateful thanks for
being here for, good heavens, can it
really be forty-eight years.

MENDOCINO

Flying Bear Press
7076 N. Aycliffe Dr.
Peoria, IL 61614
Fax. 888-881-0463

Book design by David Gregory with assistance from
Mike Brechner, Cypress House, Fort Bragg, CA

Cover design by Donna Hagerty-Payne, St Louis, MO

ISBN 978-0-9838172-0-8

Library of Congress Control Number: 2011934150

Printed in Canada

2 4 6 8 9 7 5 3 1

First edition

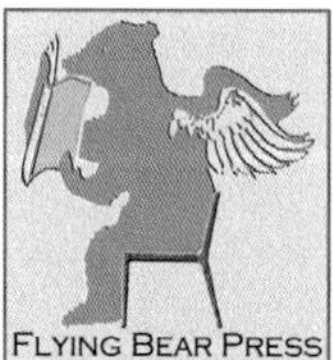

MENDOCINO

PAINTINGS BY **DAVID GREGORY** ∽ WORDS BY **JOHN BEAR**

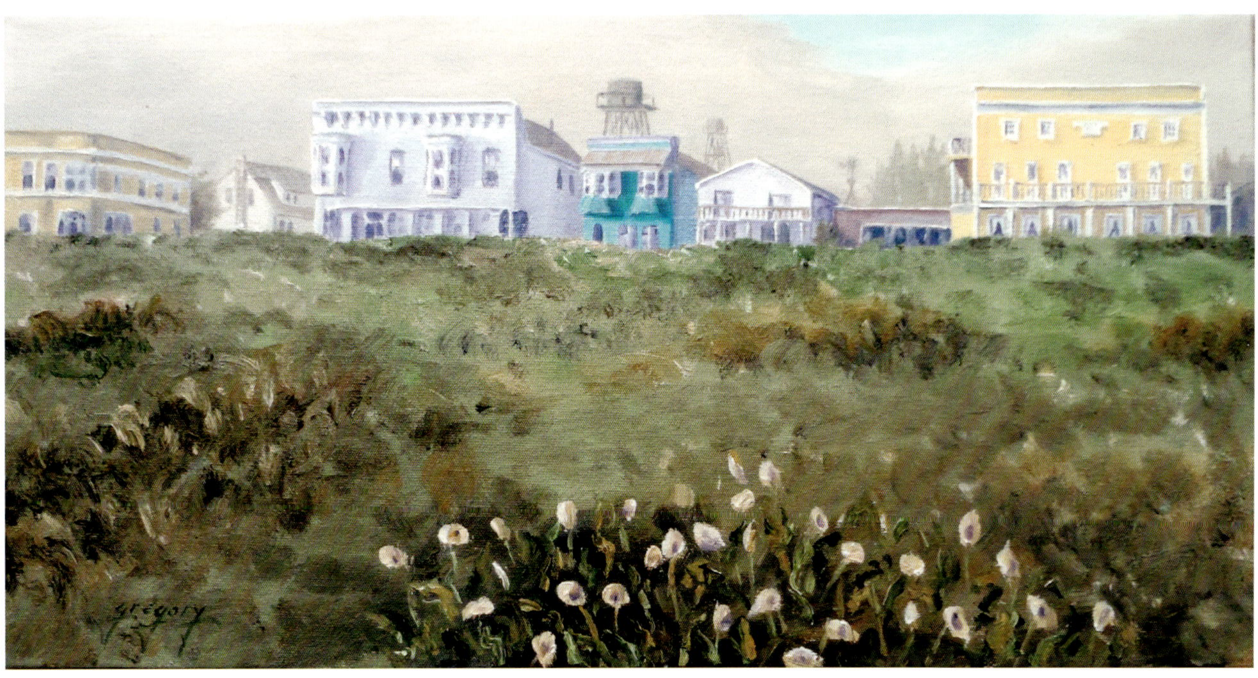

***Headlands Lilies*, oil**

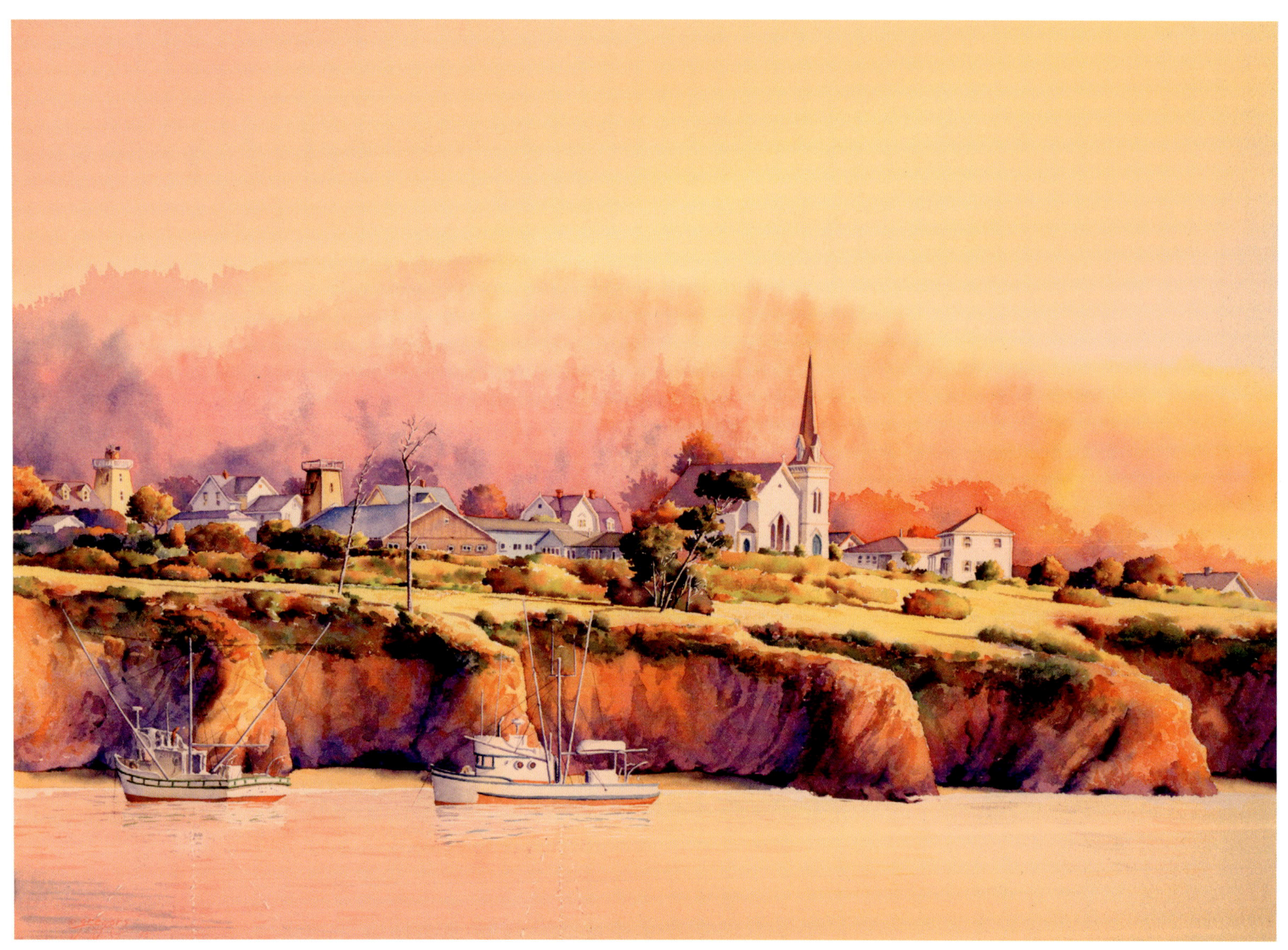

Bay View, watercolor

Oh, it is truly magical. Whether you are four hours out of San Francisco with your fingers glued to the steering wheel, or you just popped down to the Little River market to buy a bag of coffee, that first view of the Mendocino peninsula jutting out into the Pacific Ocean sets the heart astir. It is the feeling of coming home, no matter where your actual home may be. The camera and paint people should pay royalties for the Highway One turnoff near Brewery Gulch Road, the place nearly everyone "discovers" to record a quiet unhurried visual image of the town. I once saw a photographer fall off his precarious fence-post perch. His companions photographed him lying on the ground before helping him to his feet.

When you turn west from the state highway toward "downtown Mendocino" it is perhaps appropriate that the first two buildings you pass are a real estate office and a "garden" supply store. For real estate and "gardens" are two of the mainstays of the local economy and way of life. Mendocino may well have more real estate salespeople per acre than any other spot on earth. And as for the word "garden" in quotes, as Alex Trebek says, "We know what that means."

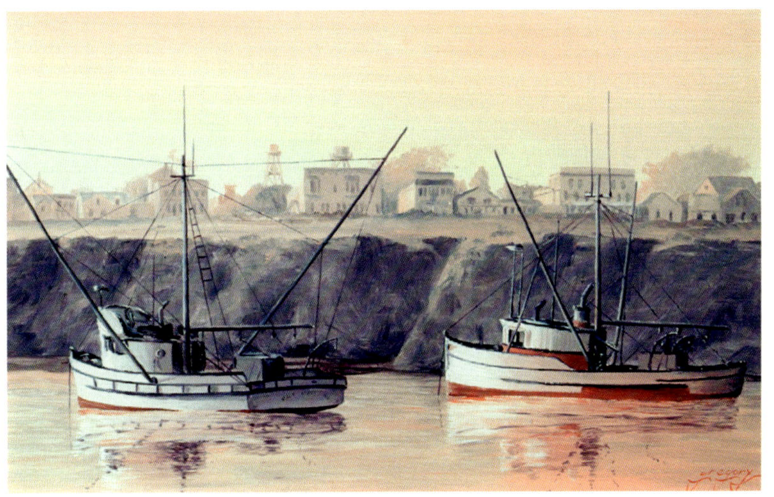

Salmon Season, oil

For a century and a half, the three major legal industries in the area have been fishing, timber, and tourism. Each in its own way has had its share of controversy and problems. The fishing industry is substantially depressed from its position a decade or two ago. There simply are not as many salmon, crabs, or albacore, as there used to be. Some blame foreign competition in the offshore waters, or pollution of the streams and rivers with debris from the timber industry, or the failure of the government to maintain price supports, or over-fishing the waters. It may have to do with any or all of these or even a natural cyclical phenomenon.

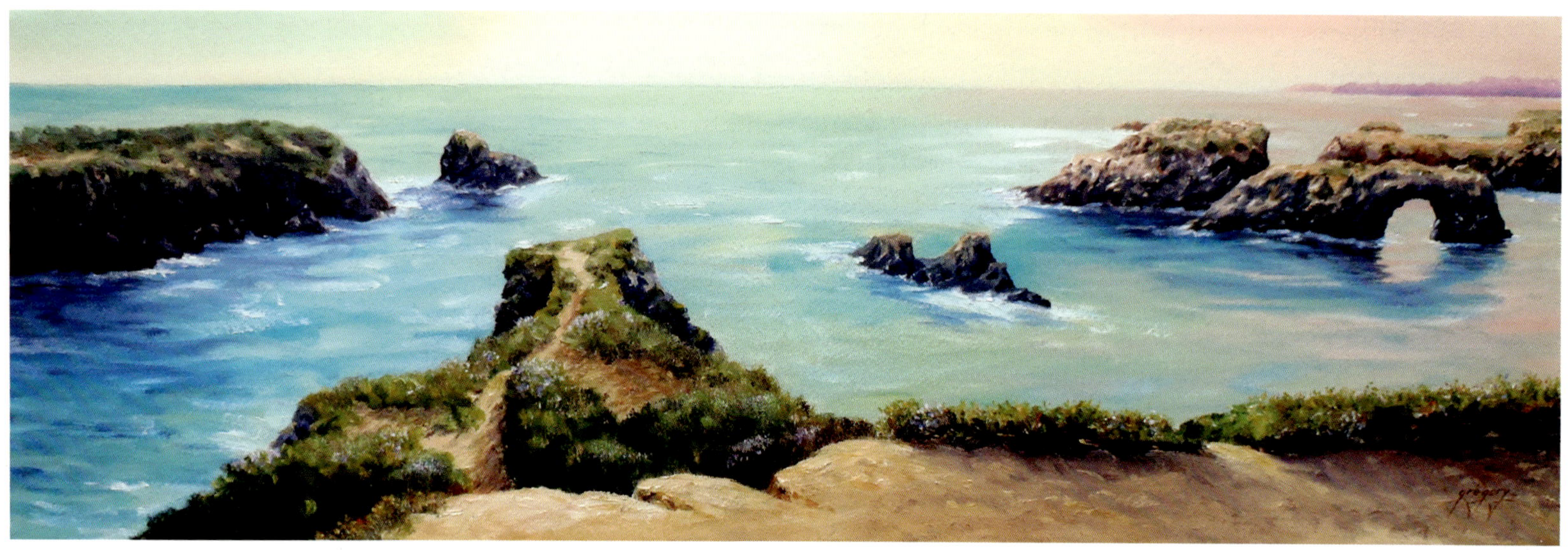

Headlands Path, oil

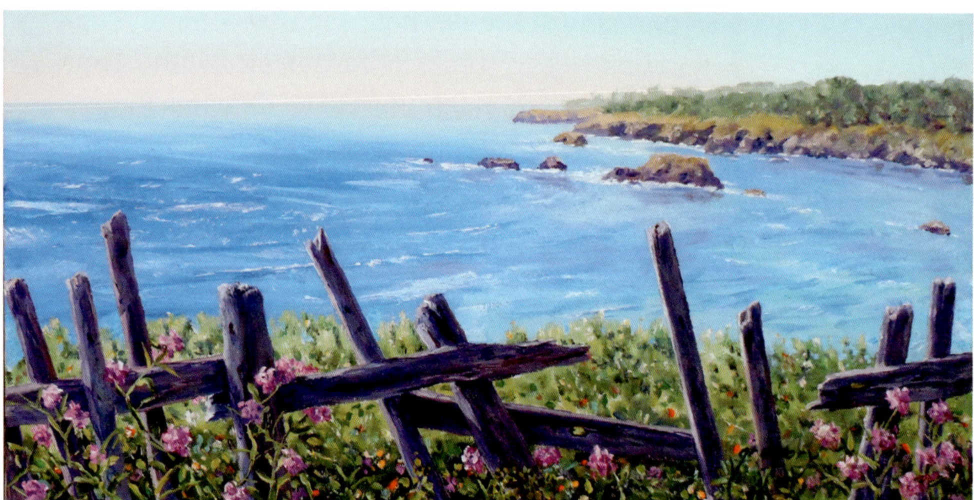

Agate Cove, oil

In the spring and fall, California gray whales can be seen spouting off Mendocino peninsula as they migrate between Alaska and their spawning grounds in Mexico. In the mid-1970s, local sculptor Byrd Baker launched a mighty campaign to "save God's whales" from the harpoons of Russian and Japanese whaling boats, some of which plied their bloody trade as close as twelve miles from the coast. The Mendocino Whale War lasted several years, and involved (among much else) a local boycott of Japanese products (it was hard to find Russian products to boycott), festivals, and a dramatic confrontation in which Baker and a few colleagues positioned themselves, in a small rubber boat, between a huge Russian whaling ship and a pod of whales. Thankfully, the Russians backed down.

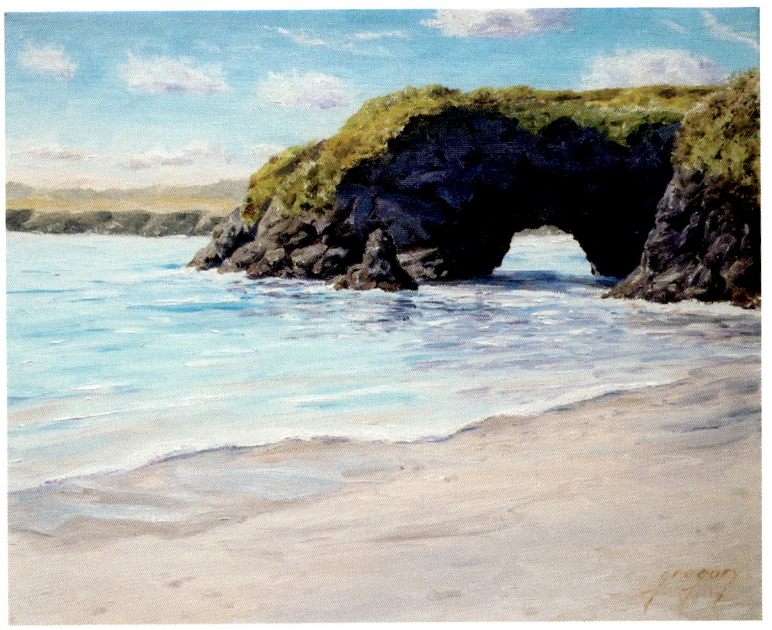

Portuguese Beach, watercolor

One of the lighter moments, good for much publicity, was a plan in which a local woman calling herself "Mendocino Rose" would go on the radio urging Russian sailors to abandon ship and come to the Mendocino headlands where she would be waiting for them with a "Russian defectors kit" (blue jeans, ball point pens, and a ticket to Disneyland). No Russians ever defected, but the Mendocino Whale War is believed to have had an impact on the eventual decision to end the killing of most whales in the northern Pacific Ocean. Indeed, a 2007 census determined, with high probability, that the 19,000-or-so whales represented the "optimum sustainable population" as defined by the Marine Mammal Protection Act. Good on you, Byrd.

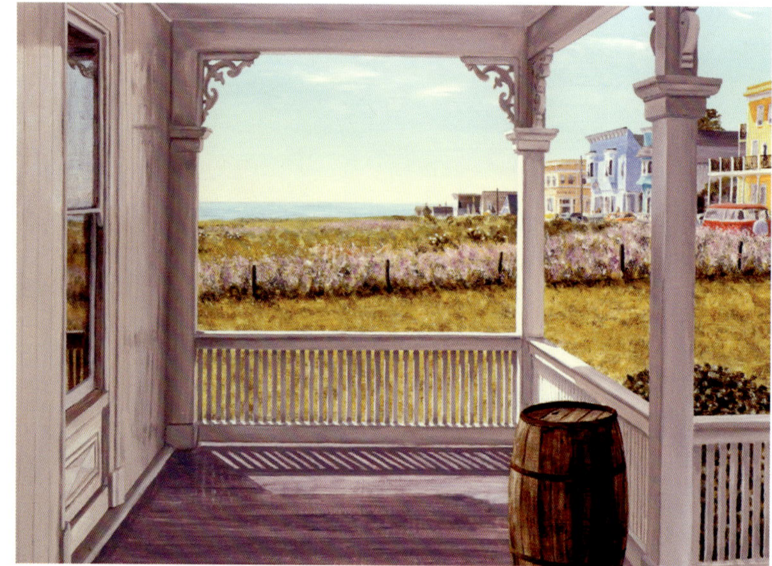

Porch View: Ford House**, oil**

J B. Ford was one of the many New Englanders instrumental in the early growth of Mendocino. He came from Connecticut in 1849, helped found the lumber mill (which lasted nearly 100 years) and in 1855 commissioned the building of what he called the Company House (we know it as Ford House) for himself and his new Connecticut bride Martha. Many locals, some respectable, some notorious, lived in Ford House after the demise of the last Ford, until it became the visitor center for the new state park.

It is an interesting exercise to buy one of the photo postcards of Main Street 100 years ago, and compare it with Main Street today. The signs on the buildings have changed, and the horses have been replaced with horseless carriages, but otherwise the differences are relatively minor.

Mendocino has managed to survive into the 21st century without a fast food franchise or a building taller than three stories. (Following a fatal accident on Highway One, however, we did get our first and only traffic light.) And yet it remains a thriving growing modern community. Behind many of those gingerbread façades lurk sophisticated computer systems, although Internet access is limited to a mile or less from town; many locals make do with extremely slow dial-up Internet service. Weathered redwood fences enclose satellite dishes. It somehow seems appropriate that Mendocino got its first computer, a state-of-the-art Digital DEC 310 with four 8-inch floppy drives and 64K of RAM, in 1974, long before it got its first elevator (in the high school gym, about ten years later). For some locals, not all of them youngsters, that elevator was a wonder of the ages; they had never ridden on one before.

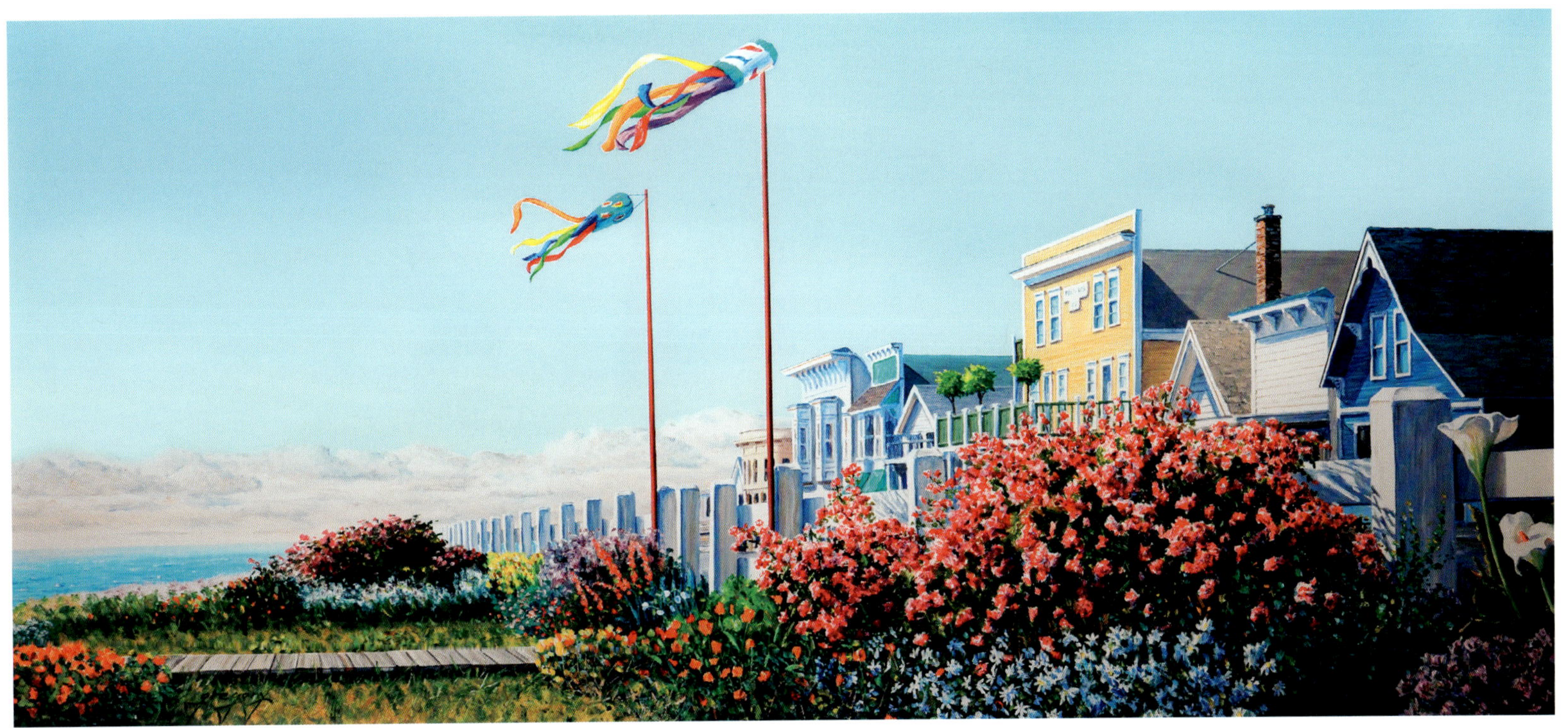

Northwest Breeze, oil

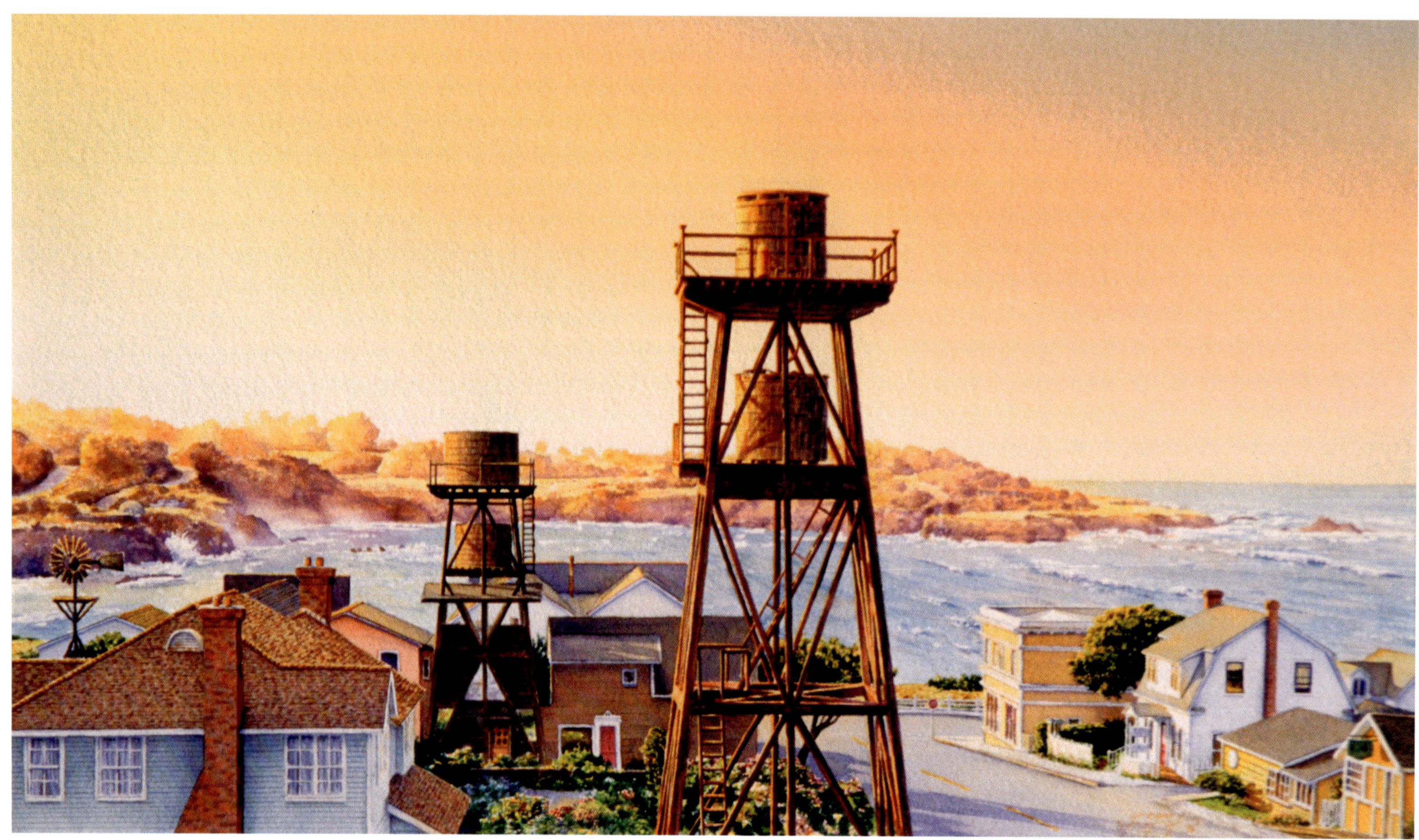

View From the Artist's Studio, watercolor

If Mendocino has a visual "trademark," it is the tall redwood water towers supported on huge beams hewn from the giant virgin growth redwoods once found nearby. Some towers were removed in the name of progress. Pumps have theoretically rendered them obsolete–but it would be hard to convince a tower owner of this when the electricity has failed (as it often does in winter storms) but the law of gravity is marching along just fine. Some towers collapsed ("demolition by neglect" is, sadly, one way to avoid costly restoration), but several new ones have appeared in recent years. The image to the left is the view from the studio where David Gregory lived and painted for a year. Can any artist in history have had a better place! The yellow building on the right was the Bank of Italy, which loaned money to victims of the 1906 earthquake, and evolved into the Bank of America.

Speaking of giant redwoods, one of those joyful 'anti entropy' events occurred in 2011 when the Save the Redwoods League raised $7.5 million and bought 426 acres of ancient redwoods near the coast, about a week before the "we will cut them all down" deadline set by the Willits Redwood Company.

Every so often, someone comes up with the idea of offering commercial air service to Mendocino, but it just doesn't work. The weather is too unreliable along the coast. Once I booked passage on the inaugural flight of a new commercial service. At 6 AM my home phone rang. "This is the airline," a voice said. "We're in San Francisco. Would you mind going outside and telling us how the weather is, so we can decide whether to fly in?" I wonder if United Airlines got it started that way?

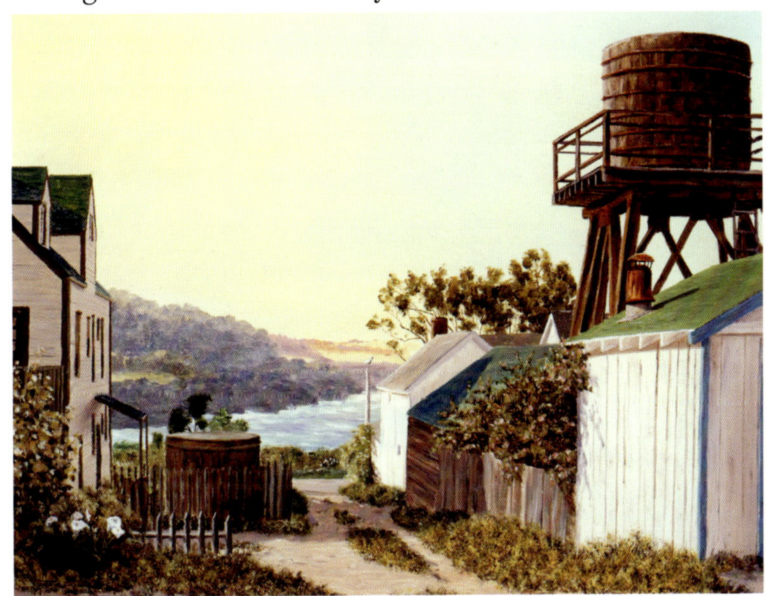

Alleyway, oil

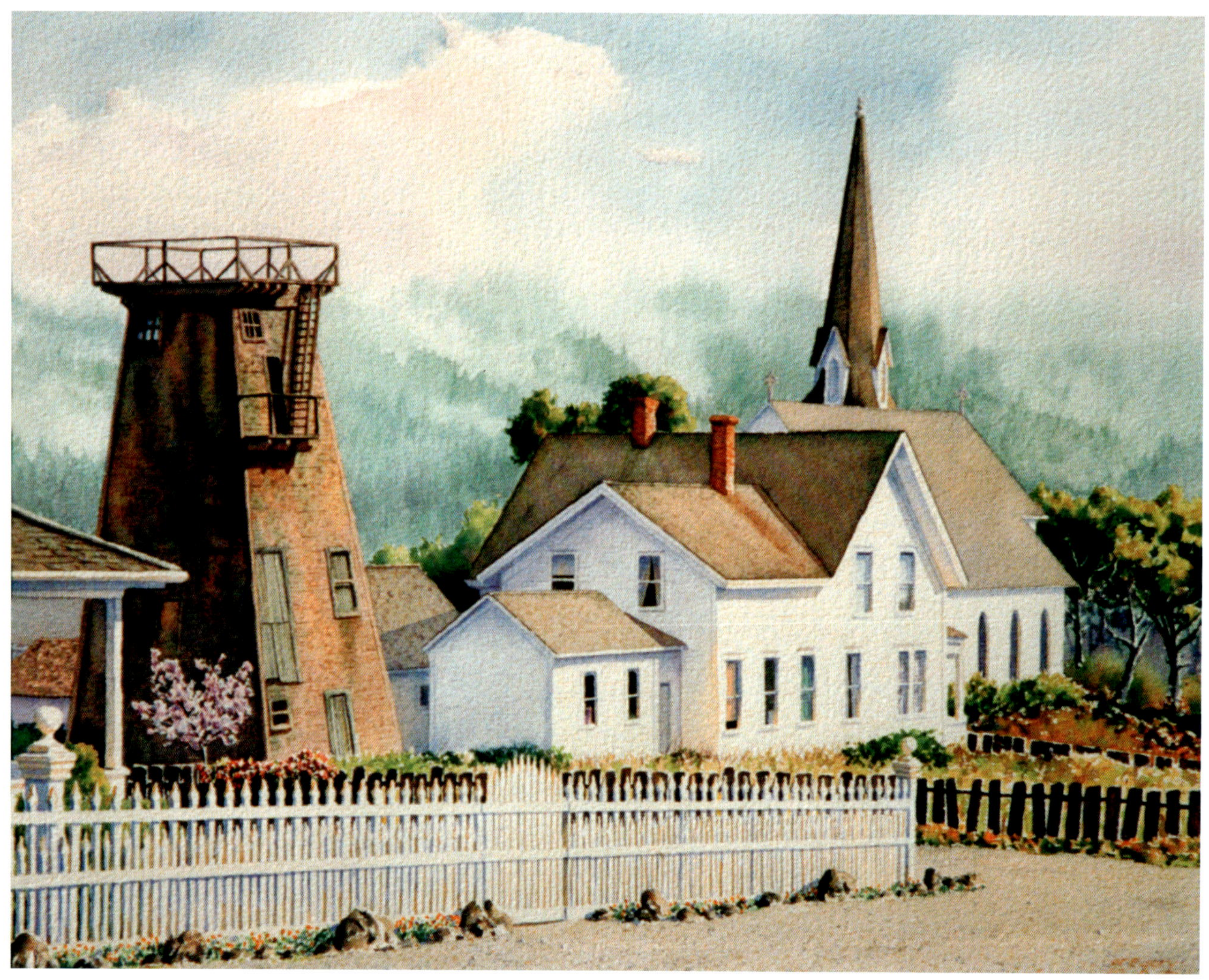

Along Howard Street, watercolor

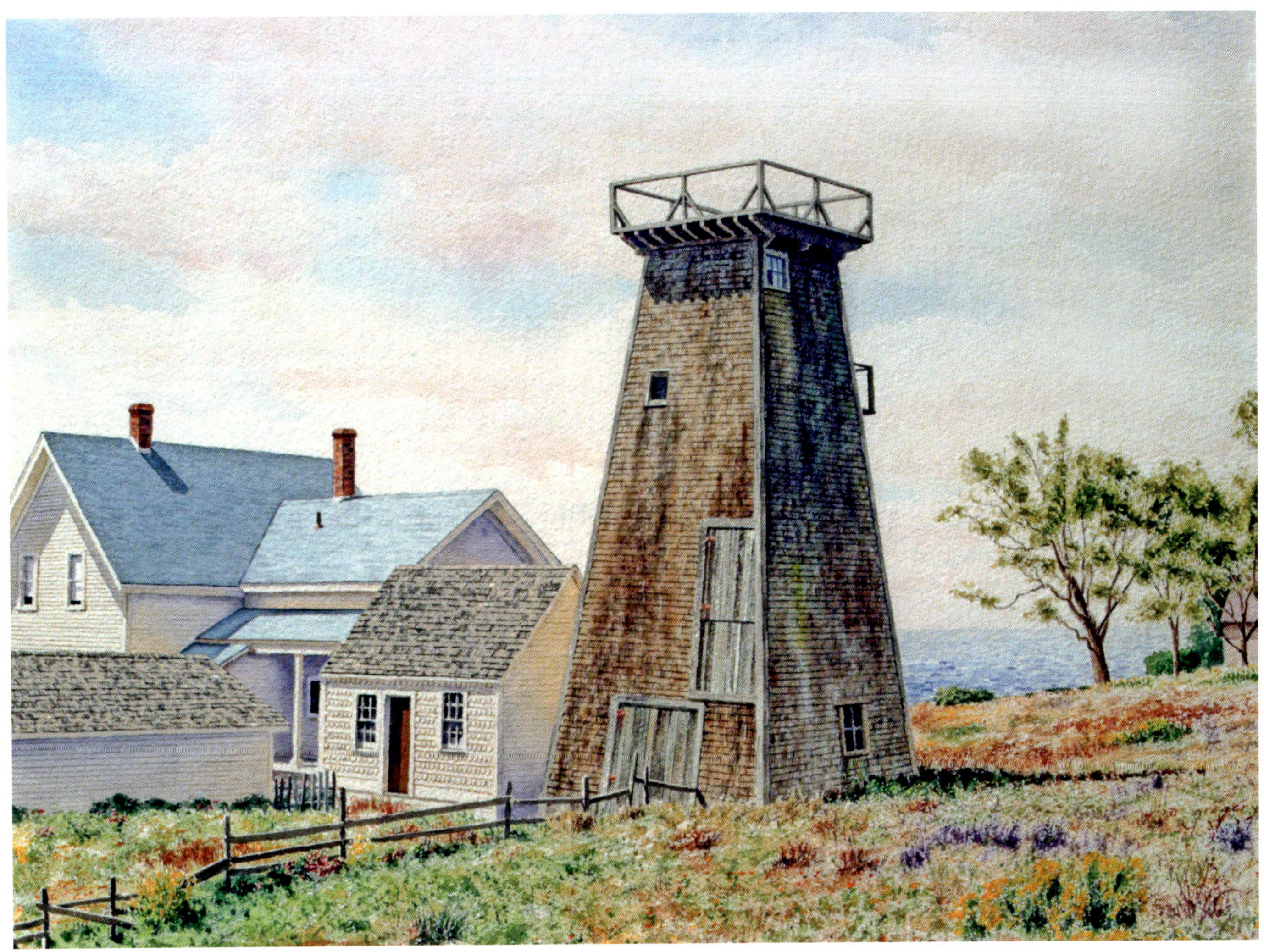

A Glimpse of the Sea, watercolor

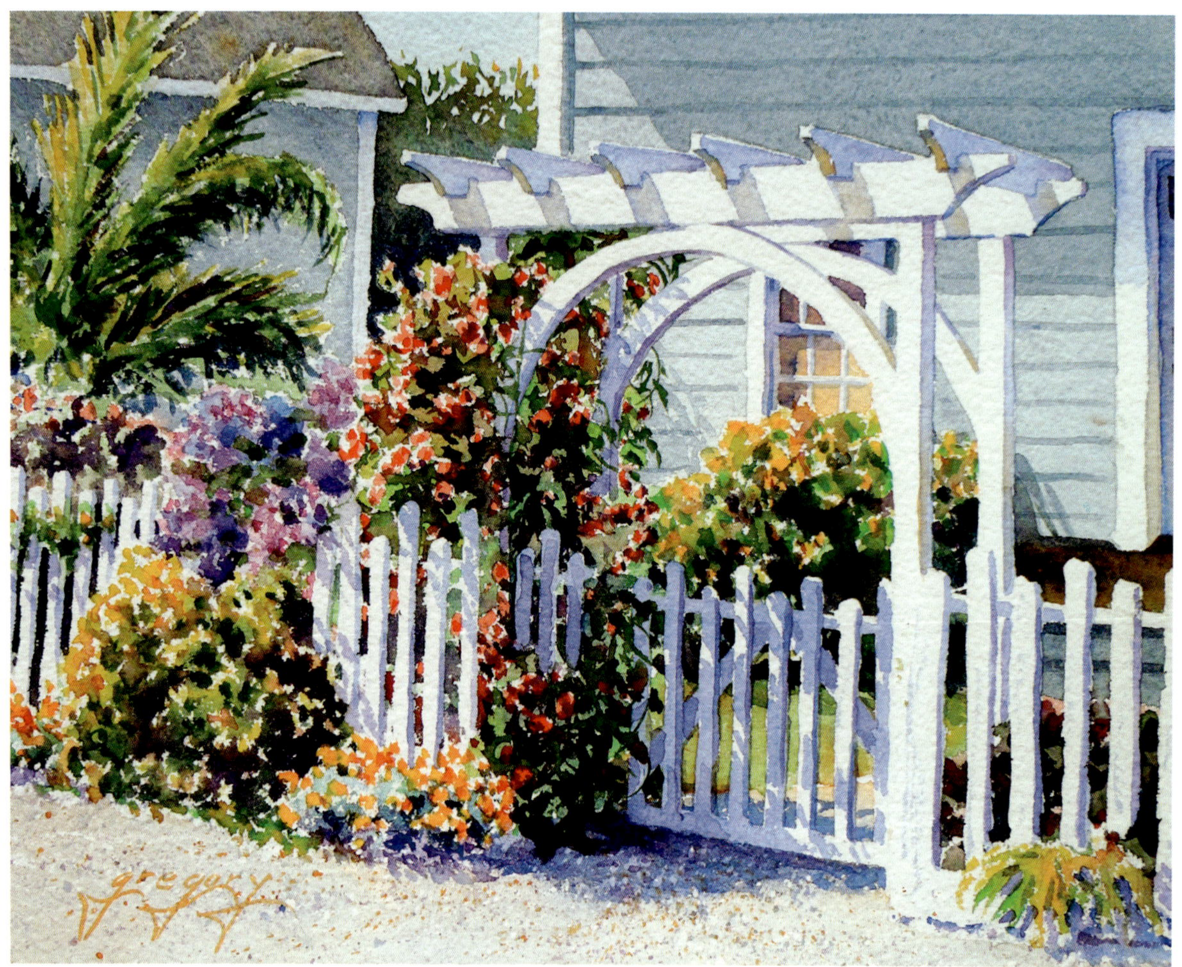

Rose Arbor, watercolor

Mendocino is special to residents and visitors alike, but a good deal of very ordinary stuff goes on here, sometimes to the surprise of the visitors. It is as if they had not expected a place as special as Mendocino to have a life of its own; to have an existence that is utterly unrelated to serving the needs of the tourists. Sort of like the time I discovered a garage sale going on at the back entrance to Buckingham Palace.

Once I saw a tourist in a classy restaurant waiting in line to use the phone. Ahead of her, her waitress was on the phone dealing with some problem with her child in school. It was apparent when the realization set in on the tourist's face that her waitress was a real human being with an independent life entirely unrelated to bringing her an herb and cream cheese omelette.

Most locals are really grateful for the tourists. It means that Mendocino City, with fewer than a thousand people can support (among much else) a dozen restaurants, a big Art Center, a theater group, an opera company, and an annual two-week-long music festival held in a huge tent on the headlands that seats more than 800 people.

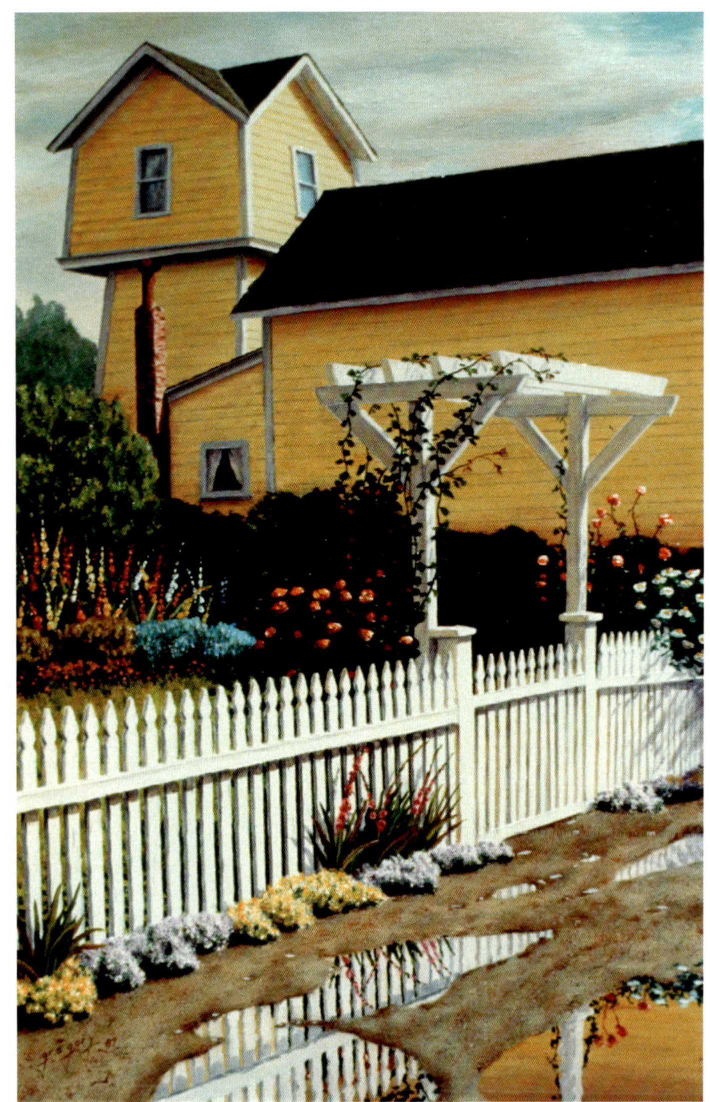

Arbor Reflections, oil

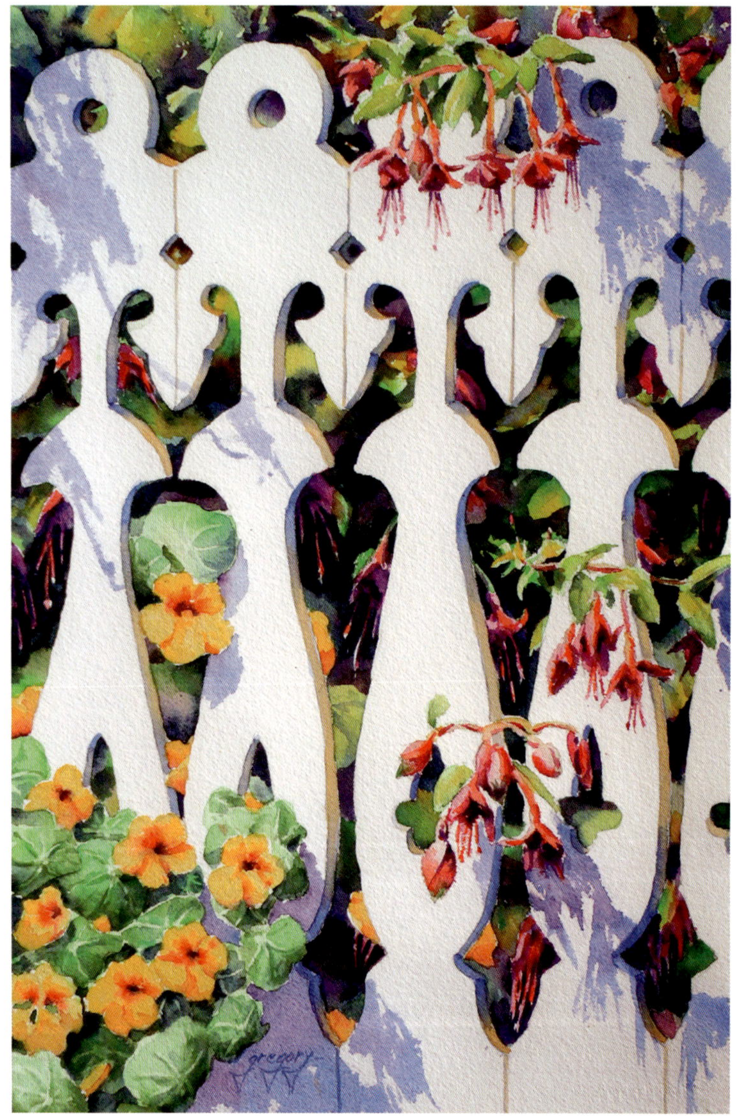

Fence & Flowers, watercolor

Fences. If good ones make good neighbors, as Frost says, the corollary, we deduce, is that bad fences make bad neighbors. Years ago, there were two adjoining property owners who got along harmoniously, if for no other reason than that one was an absentee owner who only came in to hunt or fish once or twice a year. The year-round resident erected a fence to keep the deer out of his kitchen garden. The neighbor took one look and said that first of all it was ugly, second of all it was too high, and third of all it was 18 inches onto his land.

In Mendocino, new construction is regulated by the town's Historical Review Board, the county's Planning Commission, and the California Coastal Commission. But the design and building of fences is not one of their major worries as long as no one's view is blocked. Still, before the courts got this one all sorted out, there were charges of libel, slander, defamation of character, trespass, and even attempted assault. But at least it didn't turn out to be illegal to build an ugly fence. And several decades later, the two parties still live here and are no longer enemies.

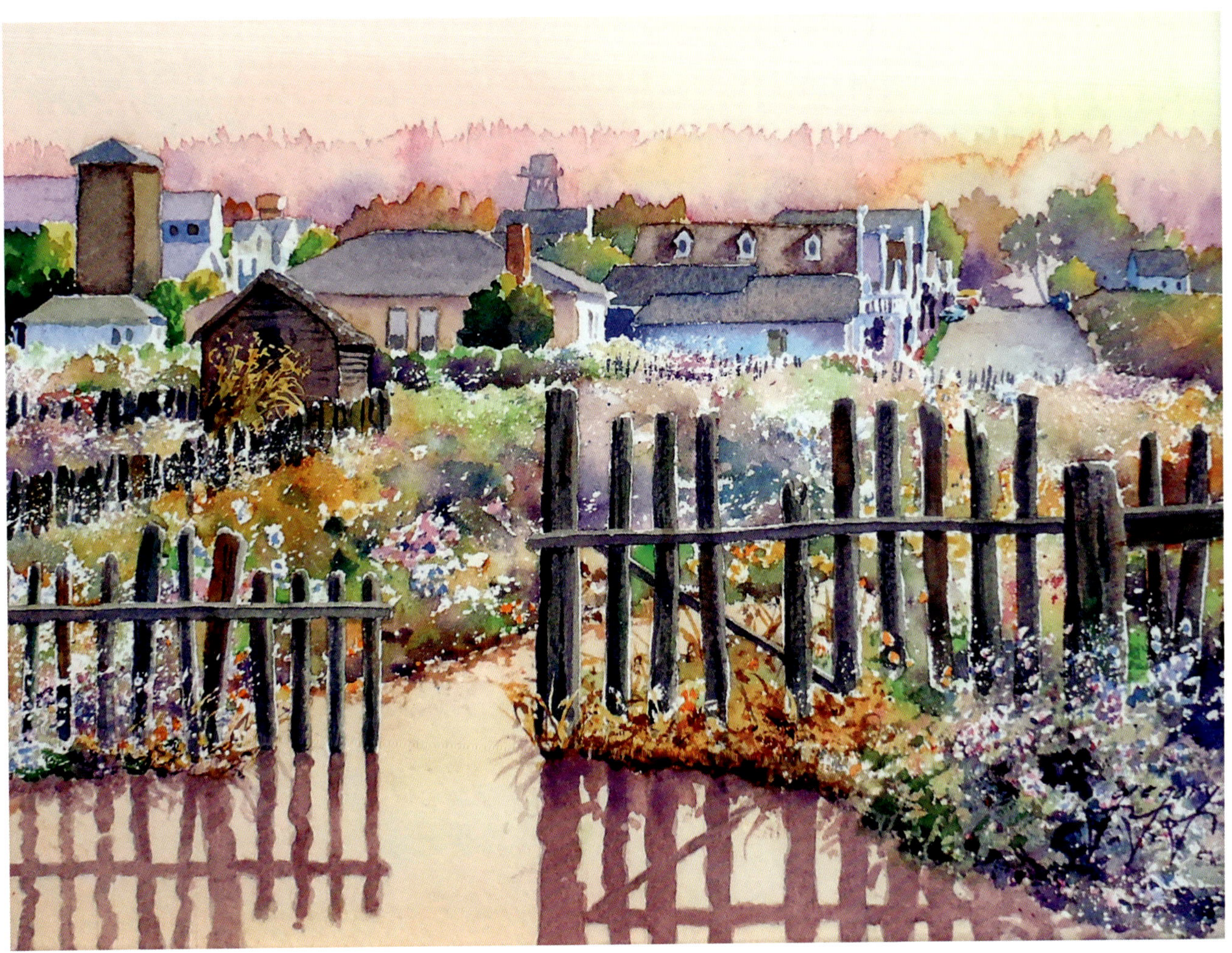

Fence Reflections, watercolor

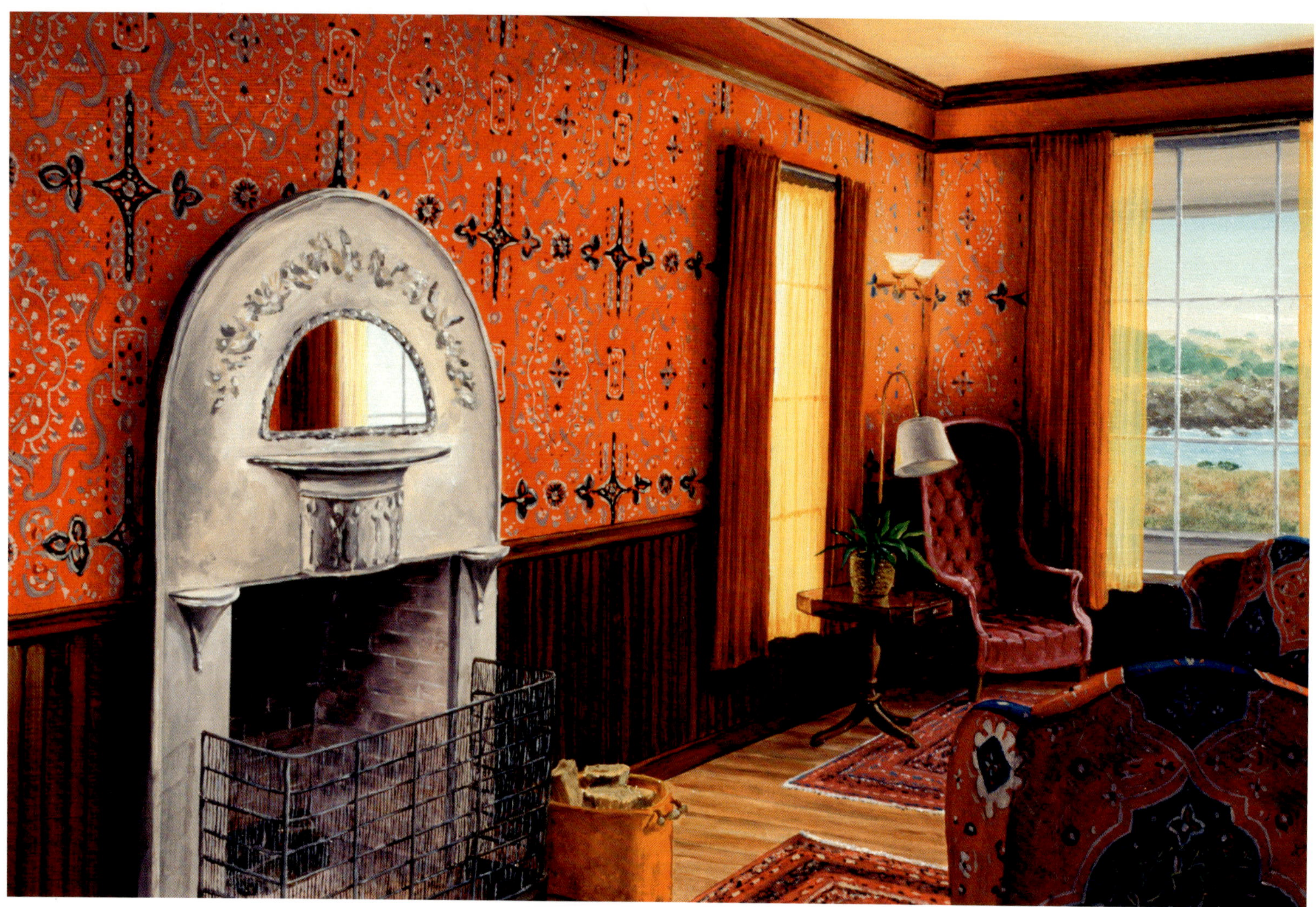

Mendocino Hotel Lobby, oil

The Mendocino Hotel is an important part of Mendocino's past, and has been a focus for a good deal of discussion about Mendocino's future. It opened in 1878 as Temperance House ("No liquor served!"). By the early 1970s it could most politely be described as funky: an ice cream stand in the middle of the lobby, and a $25-a-night bridal suite furnished, improbably, with two double beds.

It was acquired by San Diego businessman R. O. Peterson, who had grown up poor in Mendocino, and returned to invest some of his Jack in the Box fortune in an extensive remodeling of the hotel. This became the hot topic of debate that season. There were three schools of thought. One held that this was just what Mendocino City[1] needed: a boon to the local economy. Some worried that the fragile eco-system was ill-equipped to handle the increased need for water, sewage, and parking. And historical purists brought up the specter of a Mendocino theme park attraction. The bumper sticker, "Don't Carmel-ize Mendocino" appeared. Permits were issued, the work was done, and as with most burning issues of any given day, the controversy took a backseat to newer passions.

1 In our first edition, we referred to "the village," a term now being used for shopping malls. The Mendocino Community Services District and a local tide book,use the older form, Mendocino City, and so, in places here, do we.

Thomas Kravis bought the Mendocino Hotel from his brother-in-law, and has run it for decades, impressing locals with his dedication to the environment: sustainable seafood, turning cooking fat into biodiesel, low-flow plumbing, biodegradable utensils, electric car power outlets, and other green technologies.

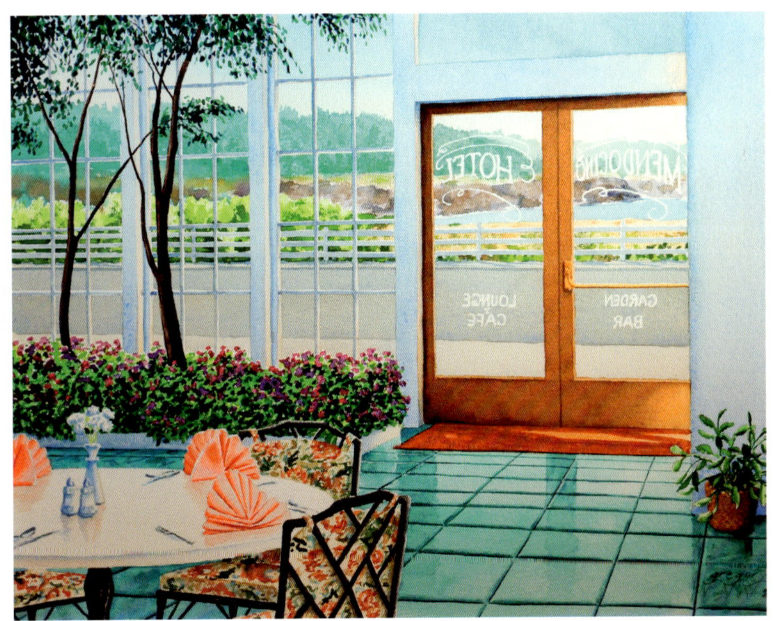

Garden Room (detail), watercolor

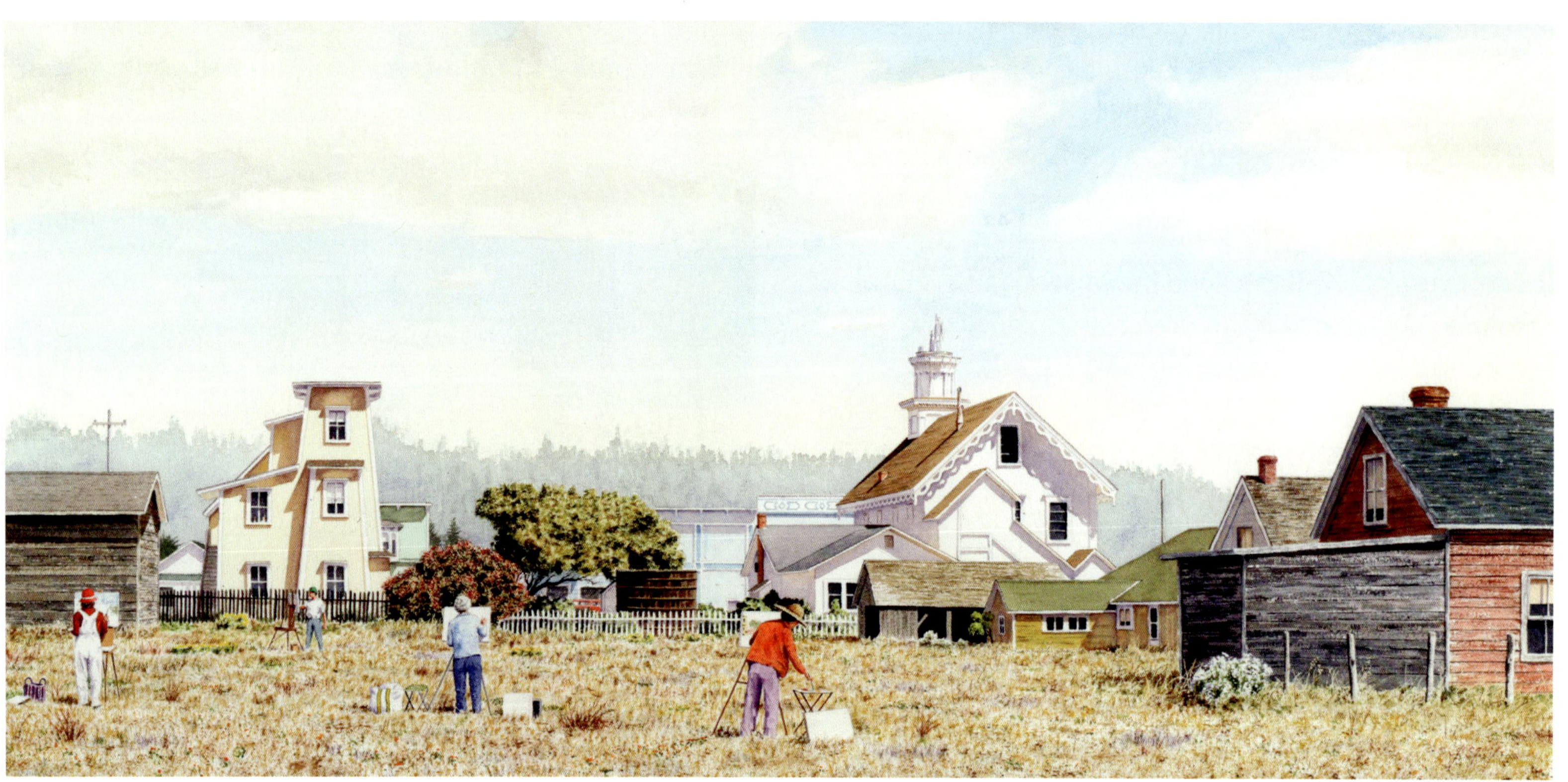

Painting Class, watercolor

The Mendocino Land Trust has done wonderful work since 1976 in saving and preserving more than 11,000 acres of local land, including two very important acres known as Heider Field, in the center of town.

In the 1970s, resident John Heider tried and failed to get the necessary permits to open a school for human potential. When he finally gave up, he donated the land to the local Presbyterian church.

As it happened, there was some state park land adjoining the church. The Mendocino Land Trust brokered a clever deal, in which the State Parks traded their land near the church for Heider Field, and then turned it over to the Trust for management. Now it is one of the prime open spaces in town, used for an annual street fair, May Pole dancing, and other community events. On May Day, a group of locals sometimes stands in Heider Field and unfurls a large banner reading, "Hurray, hurray, the first of May. Outdoor [rude word] begins today."

Much of the intricate "gingerbread" work on the balconies and trim dates from the mid-to late 19th century, but there is also much that is newly created by local

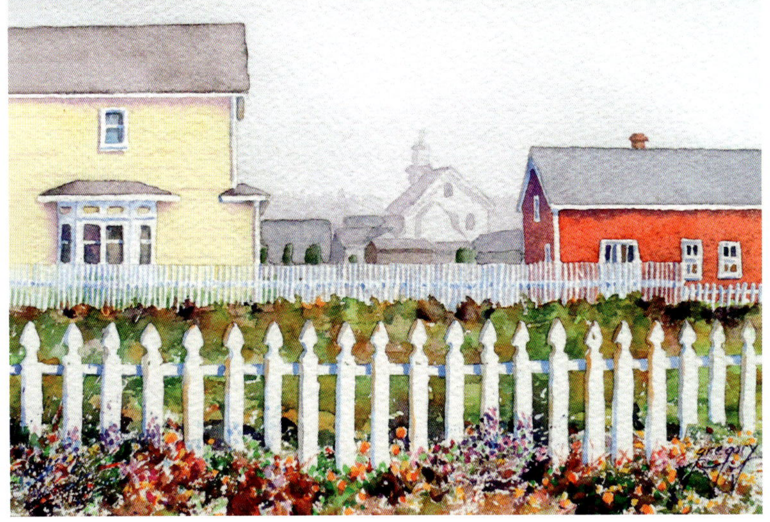

Picket Fences, watercolor

woodworkers. New construction is more likely to get the needed permits if the design is compatible with, but not an exact copy of something old.

In their lovely book of photographs of historical Mendocino, Dorothy Bear and Beth Stebbins write that the style has "been classified as Gothic Revival, Saltbox, Gingerbread, Rustic, Pointed Cottage, Carpenter's Gothic, and once in a while just plain awful."

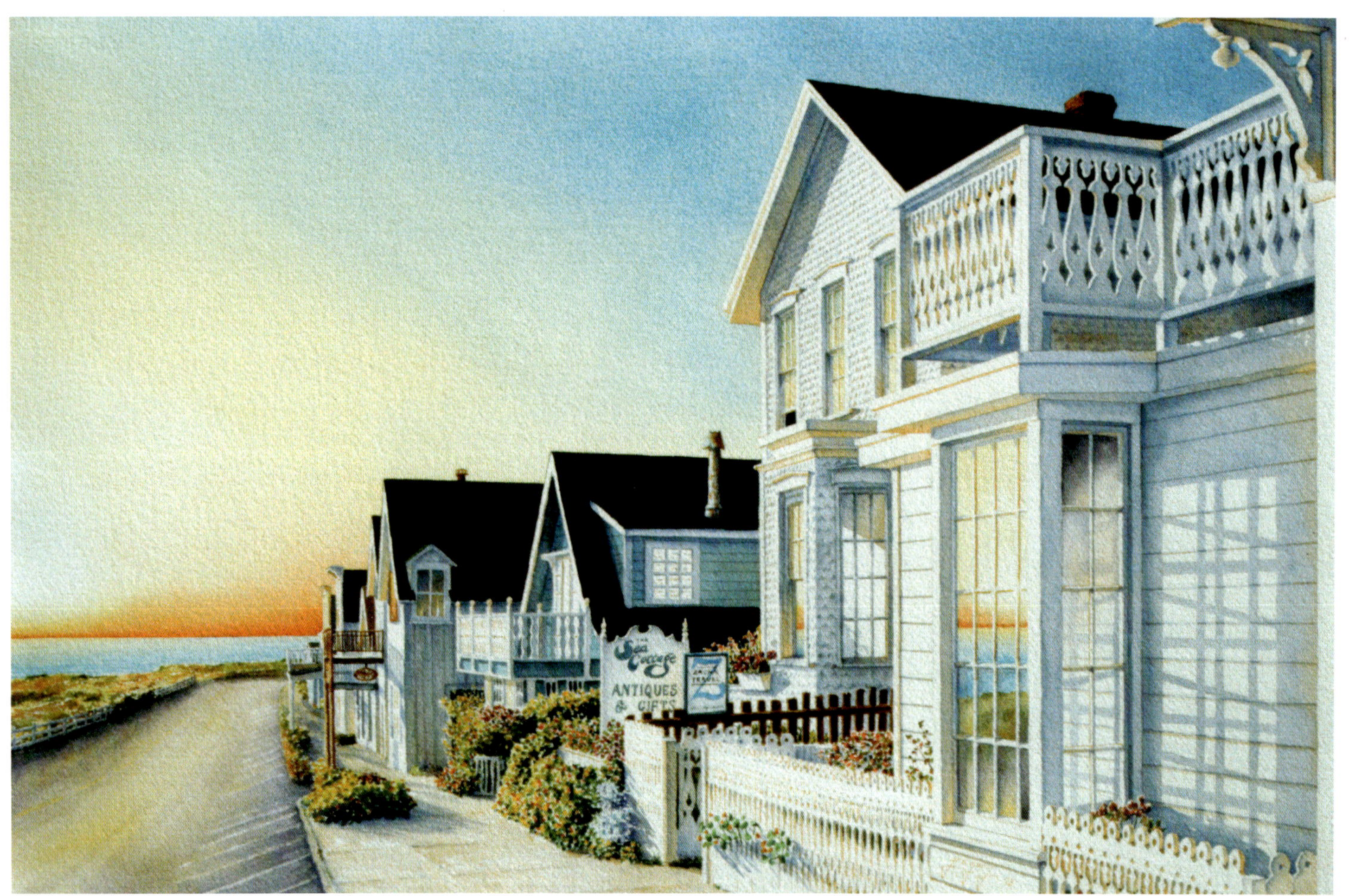

Sunset Reflections, watercolor

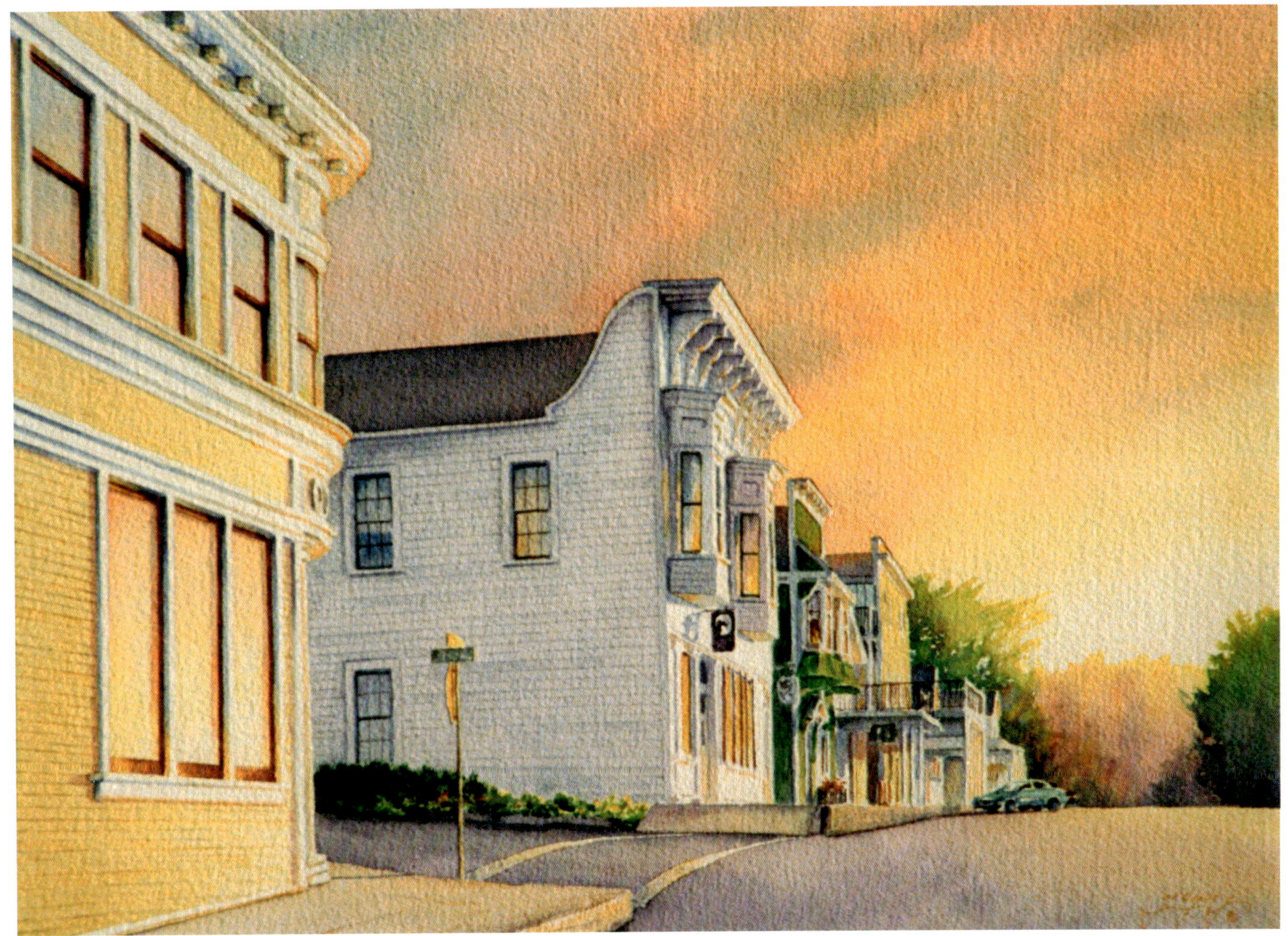

Main Street Morning, watercolor

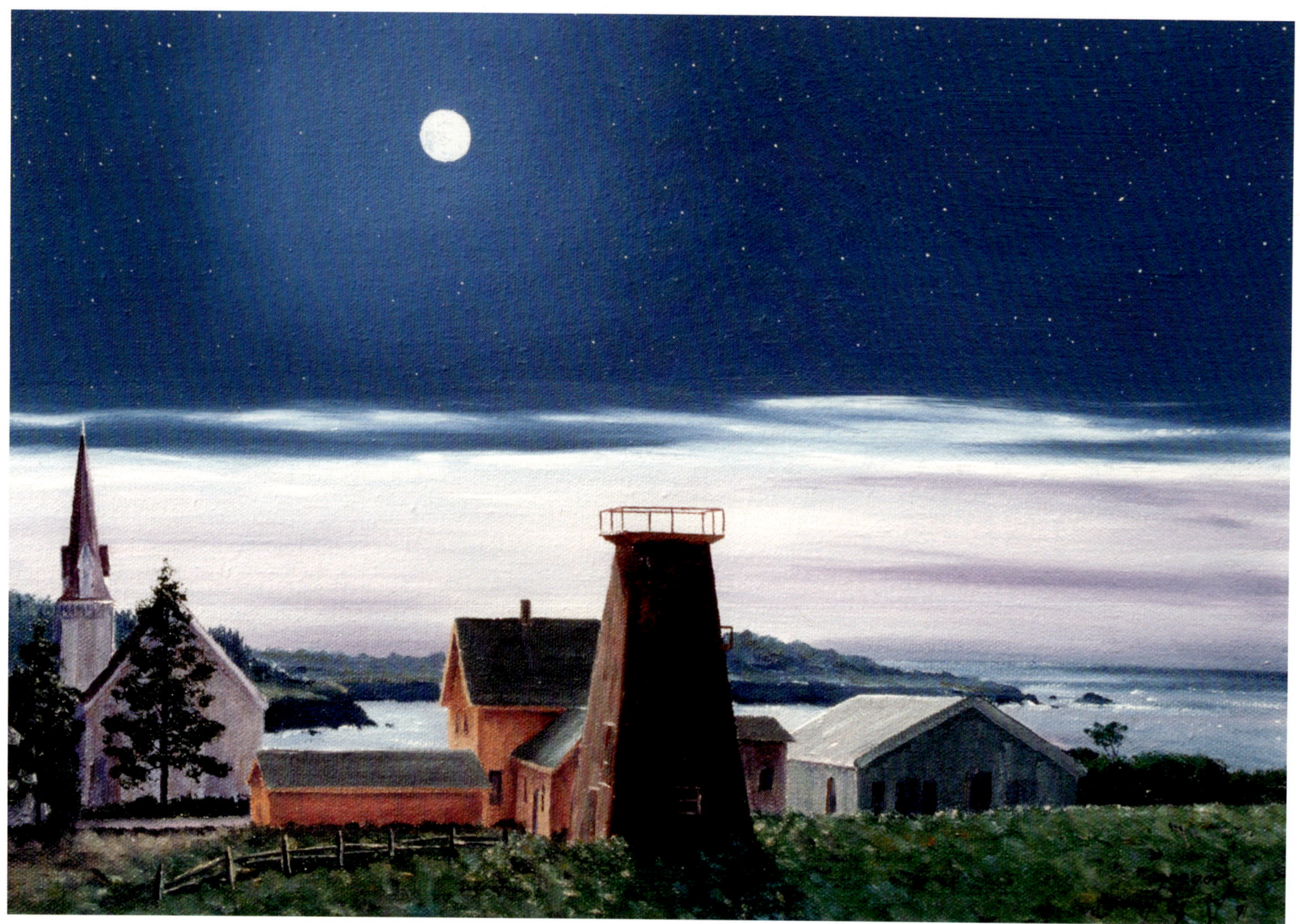

Moon Over Mendocino, oil

Our eldest daughter, Mariah, went straight from 11th grade at Mendocino's alternative high school to an alternative sort of university (Evergreen State), but only lasted a year there. "Going out under the full moon and leaping in the air shouting 'Yafatah!' Been there, done that. Don't need more of it," she said. She transferred to that nice conservative university in Berkeley and graduated Phi Beta Kappa three years later.

It was because of Mendocino High School that our family left Mendocino the first time. More accurately, *one* of the Mendocino high schools, since this sparsely-populated area has four of them: regular, alternative (started in the 1970s as an outreach to the youth of the area who had dropped out of the regular schools and the system), community, and vocational. Our twin daughters had their first real taste of life outside Mendocino when they were in 9th grade and we traded houses with a Berkeley family for a few weeks one summer. They loved it, and began plotting and planning, leading up to a presentation one Sunday morning. The gist of it: "You folks are so big on education. Why must we go to a tiny rural school with minimal science and foreign language education? We want to go to Berkeley High." The time seemed right, after ten years in Mendocino, so off we went. And then they pulled the old switcheroo. In 9th grade, they passed the G.E.D. exam and went on to college — one at once, one after working for a few years.

Our local college, College of the Redwoods, is a small branch of the main campus in Eureka, a three-hour drive on challenging roads, to the north. There has long been a tense dynamic between the local campus, wishing to serve better the needs of the coast, and the main campus, widely felt to be out of touch with the locals. This was made abundantly clear in 2010 when the president declared that coastal people didn't have "a proper mindset" to receive higher education. When it was learned that said President had applied for a job in a far-away district, more than a few local people wrote enthusiastic unsolicited letters of recommendation on his behalf, and there was a feeling of relief when he resigned a few months later to take that other job.

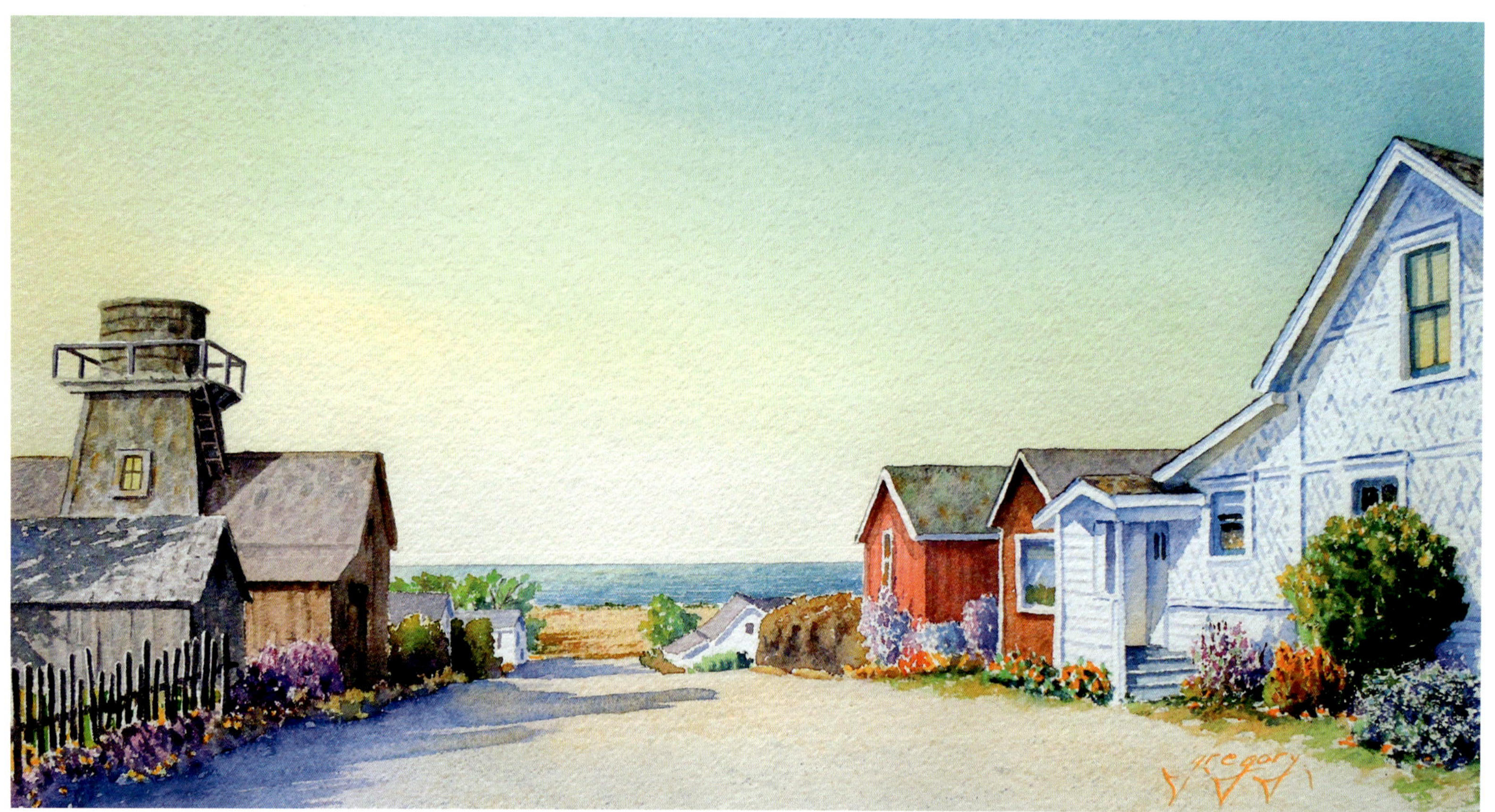

Calpella Street View, watercolor

Mendocino, for most intents and purposes, does not exist. That is not a metaphysical remark, but a legal one. Mendocino has never incorporated as a city; it is simply a part of Mendocino County. Its laws are passed and administered by the County supervisors (a 90 minute drive away in Ukiah). Its police force is the County Sheriff and his deputies.

For many people in Mendocino that's just fine. The system works and they do not wish to tamper with it. For others it is unconscionable that five supervisors, only one of whom is from the Mendocino area, should make and enforce their laws.

Every decade or so, the matter of incorporation becomes a hot topic, and every so often, it finds its way onto the ballot.

In 1882, the matter arose and virtually cleaved the town in two. There were heated arguments, fisticuffs, and a barrage of letters to the editor. Some said "Let us gain control of our destiny." Others said, "We have enough government already." In the end, nothing came of it until exactly 100 years later when a vote was held and incorporation won by two votes. But wait! Four absentee ballots were discovered, and now incorporation lost by two votes, and there it stands. There seems much more interest in changing the name of the town to the north from its 'honoring' an undistinguished and generally unsuccessful and unpopular Confederate general, Braxton Bragg (who never saw the place), to the original Indian name of Noyo ... or almost anything else.

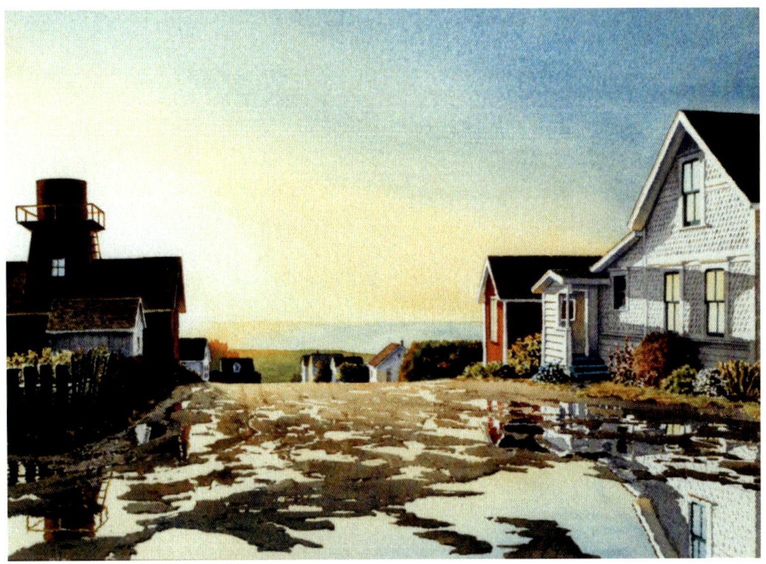

After a Storm, watercolor

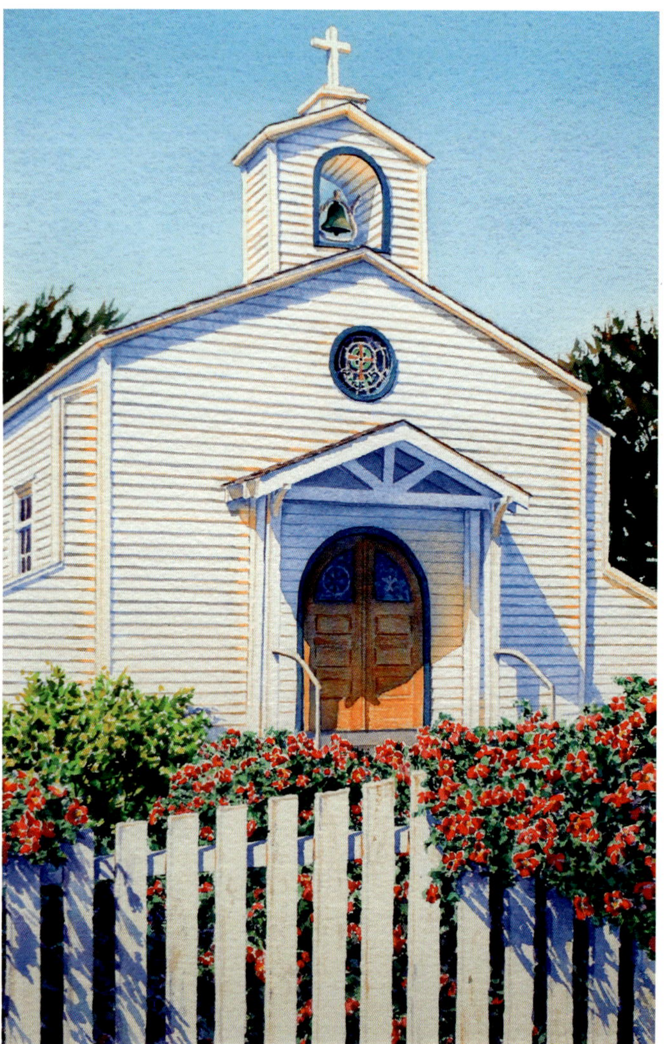

St Anthony's, watercolor

St. Anthony's was built in 1930 to replace an 1864 church that had burned. It is on Cahto Street, which in old books is "Catho" street. Typographical error or odd coincidence? Something to ponder as you sit in the weekly bingo game.

Downhill from St. Anthony's is a big yellow building with an odd history. It was originally a classroom building on the high school campus across the street, marked for demolition to build a new gym. People wanted to save it, but the only place it could be moved was to the grounds of St. Anthony's, an unlikely prospect. But wait! It turned out that years before, the church, needing money, had sold half its land to Berkeley publisher Phil Wood, publisher of many of John Bear's books. A deal was struck. Bear bought the building from the school district for a dollar and traded half of it to Wood for half his land.

Many people turned out one cold Sunday morning to watch the 40 by 80-foot building deftly rolled across the street by skilled house movers. Subsequently Bear and Wood donated it to the school district for use by the vocational high school and MCN, the network service owned and operated by the District.

A British visitor to Mendocino once scoffed, "Why your so-called ancient church is barely 100 years old. Back home that would be thought of as new." Well, it's all relative, isn't it. Consider that this splendid edifice, made of native redwood locally milled, was built in 1868, less than two decades after the first non-Indian settler, William Kasten, was shipwrecked off the nearby coast.

The Presbyterian Church of Mendocino is one of the oldest Presbyterian churches in California and probably the most photographed. While the church and its members play an important role in the spiritual and social life of the community, even those who do not belong seem to take comfort from the solid, traditional landmark. It simply looks the way a church should look. The inside, however, is quite unexpected. Check it out, sometime.

By the end of World War II, the church was badly in need of repair. To the rescue came the makers of the movie *Johnny Belinda* (starring Jane Wyman, the then-Mrs. Ronald Reagan), filmed in and around the church in 1947. The fees they paid enabled the elders to bring the building to the condition in which you see it today.

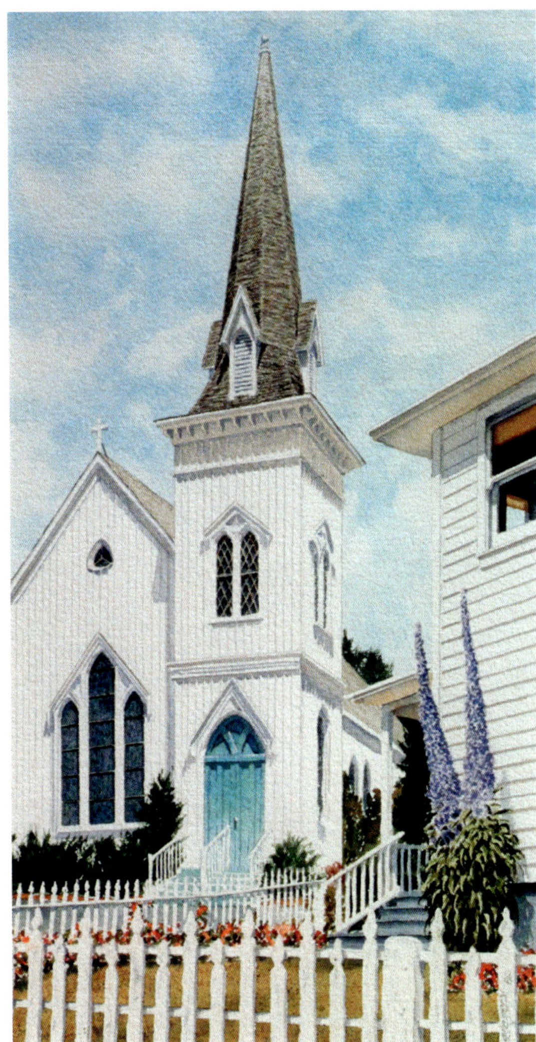

Presbyterian Church, watercolor

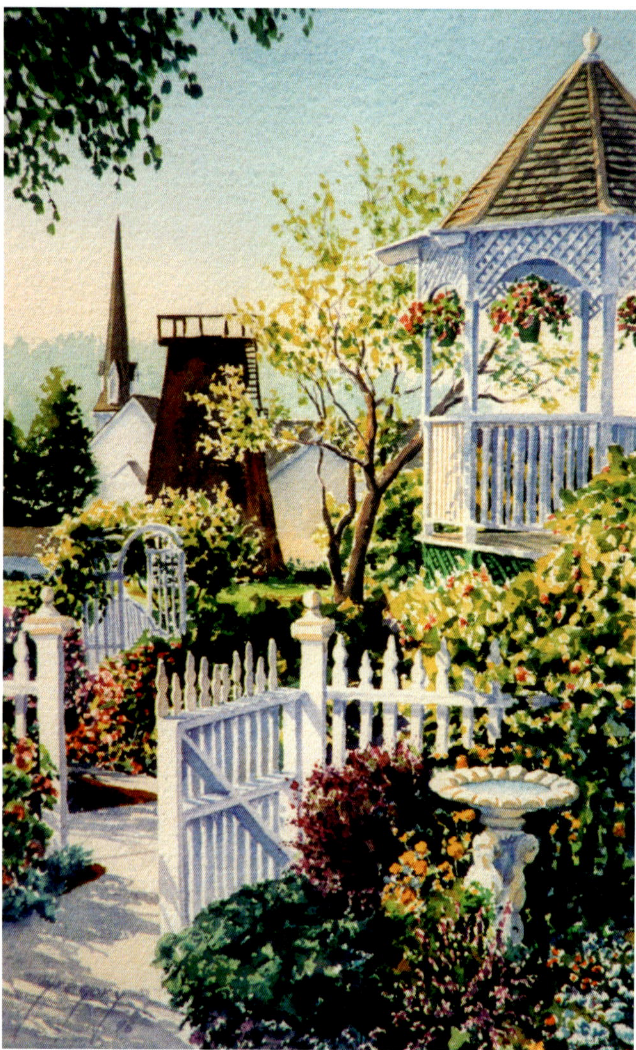

Gazebo Garden, watercolor

David does not have a new image of Heritage House, one of the most painted places on the coast, but there are a few things to be said, as it affects the future of the whole area. Heritage House used to be an elegant array of oceanfront cottages, and quite possibly the only place within a hundred miles of Mendocino with a dress code. The play *Same Time Next Year* was written with Heritage House in mind, and the Alan Alda movie was filmed there. In the mid 2000s, the complex was bought by investors with a plan to turn it into "eclectic rooms" for "Asian kingpins" to have "meditative experiences." Those kingpins will have to meditate elsewhere, because Heritage House closed for good in 2008 amid charges of malfeasance and fraud, followed by a "no contest" plea by the principal investor. The German bank that was financing the deal foreclosed on the loan, and there were no bids in a subsequent auction. What happens next with this multimillion-dollar oceanfront property is is bound to have an impact on the coastal economy and growth plans. Something for the "kingpins" or something for the locals? At press time, there were encouraging rumors of a plan to turn it into an elder hostel.

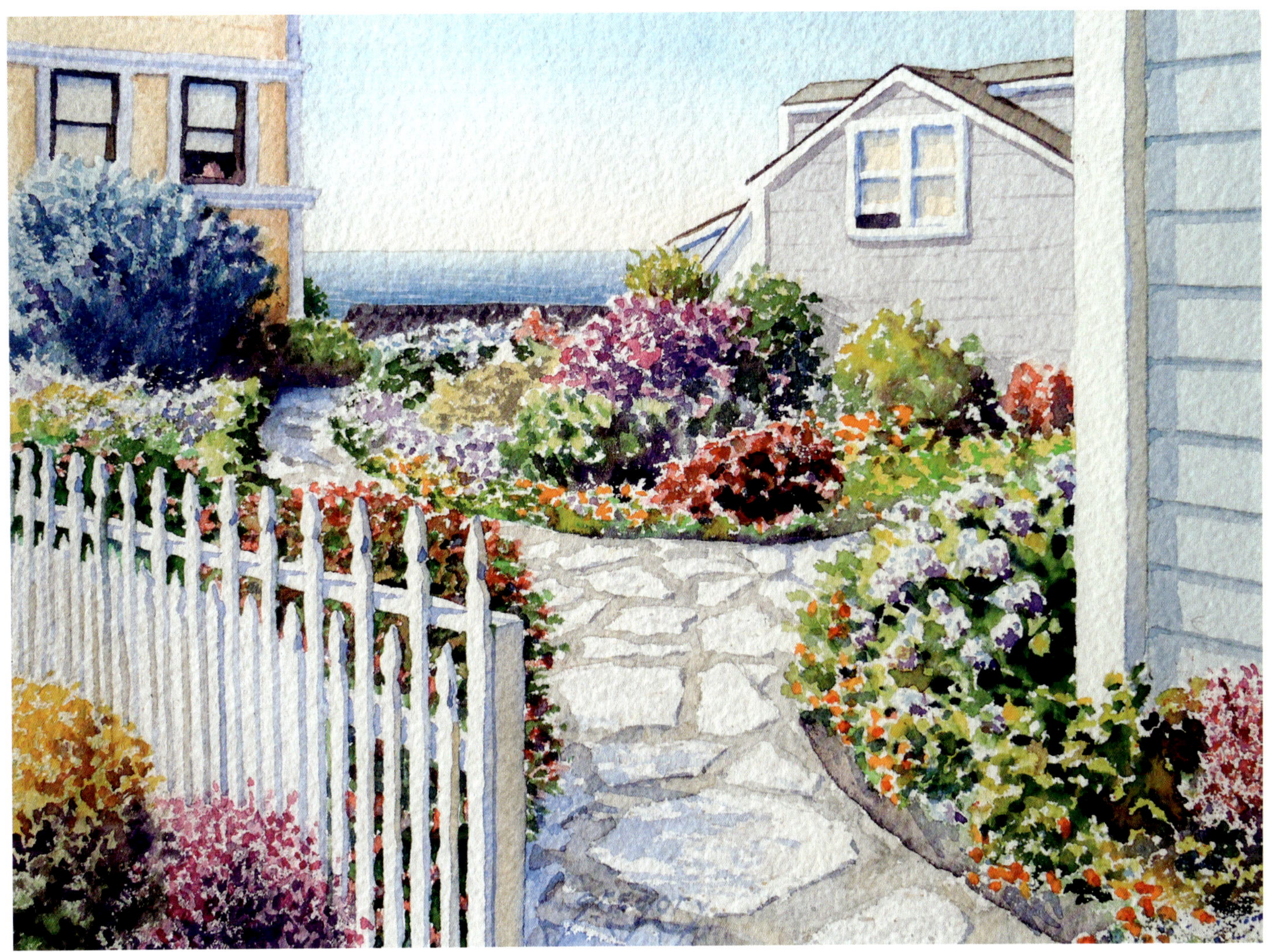

Garden Path, watercolor

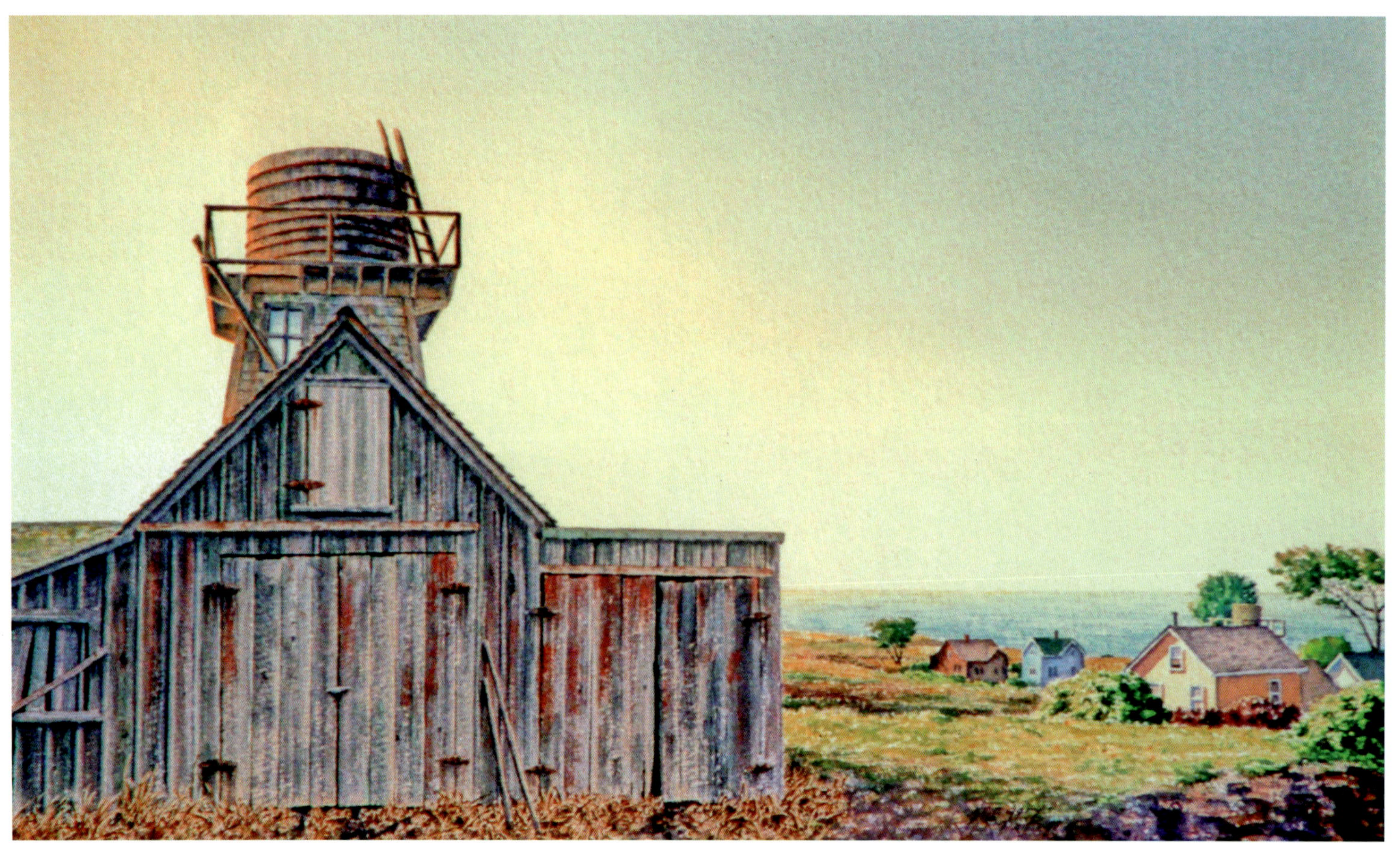

Morning Light, watercolor

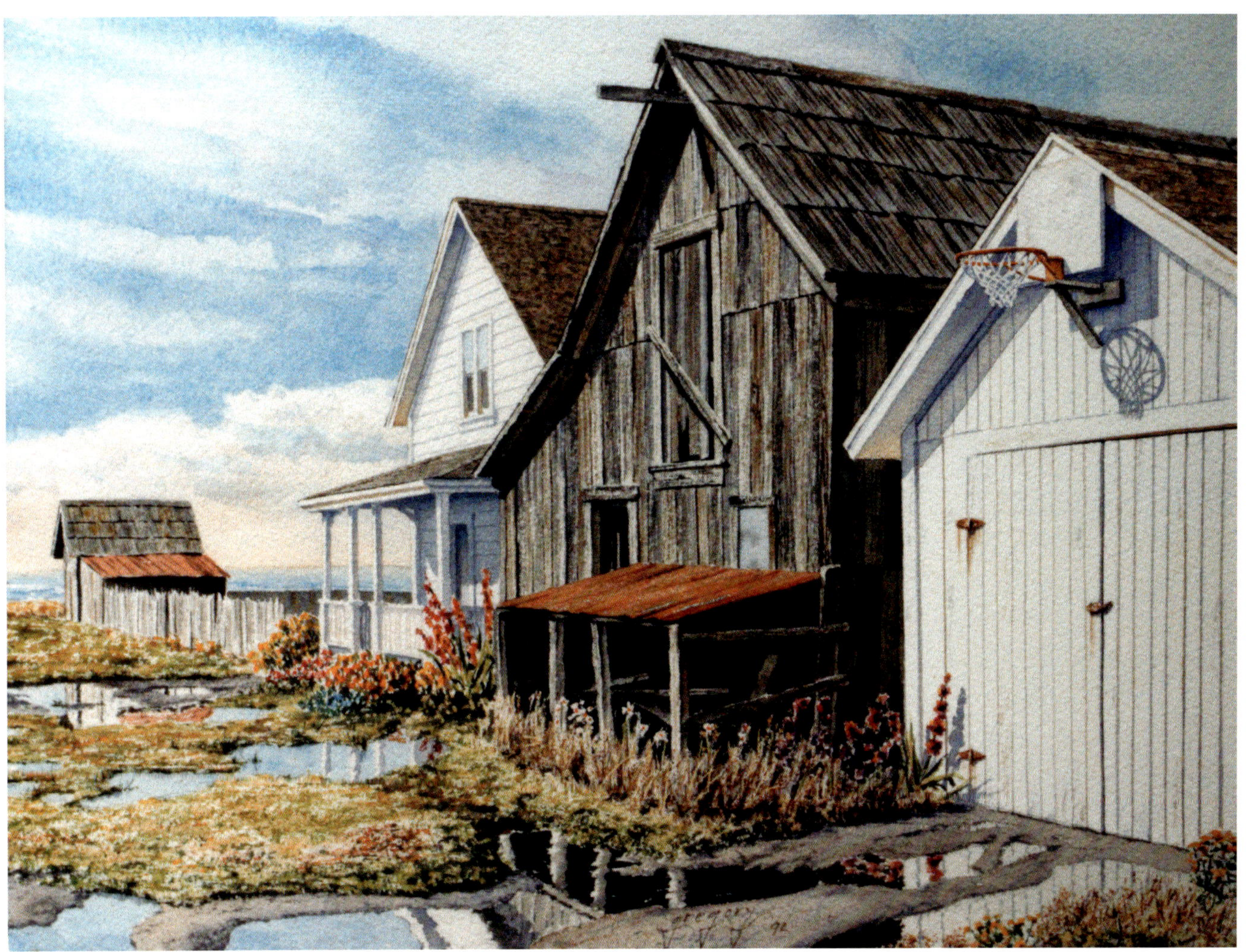

Passing Storm, watercolor

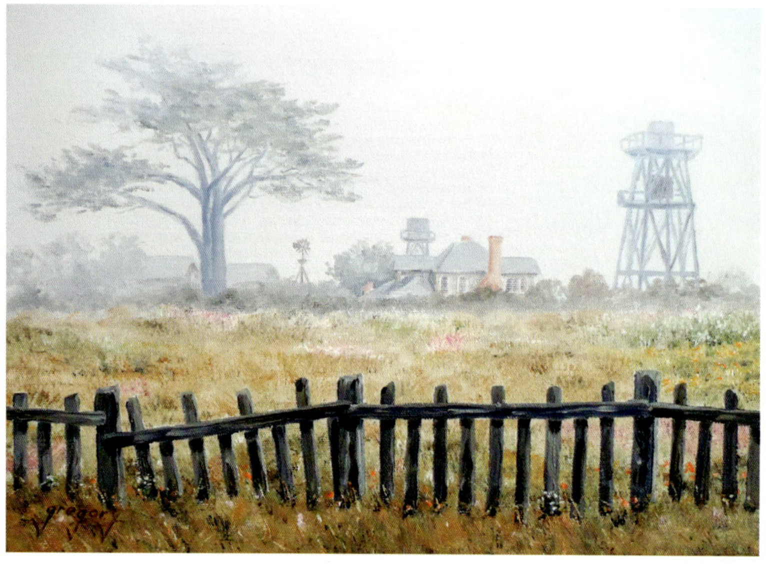

Morning Fog, oil

One of the unexpected things about Mendocino weather is that you can often see it before it gets here. Weather fronts move in from the west or the northwest. It is not uncommon on a bright and sunny day, to look west and there, out over the ocean, is a huge fog bank or even a rainstorm, poised to move in over the town. There have been times when, for a brief period, there was a heavy rainstorm on our back deck and it was clear and pleasant in front of the house.

As with many rural communities, weather is an important factor in the life of Mendocino–more so because of the geographical isolation. Local radio station KZYX says their frequent weather reports are their most popular program. There are only three paved roads into Mendocino—one from the north, one from the east, and one from the South—and there have been times when all three were closed by fallen trees, flooding, or landslides. And flooding doesn't just mean a few puddles on the road. On Highway 128 leading south toward San Francisco, there used to be a watermark sign 12 feet up on a pole, showing where the water level had gotten to in one particular storm. The sign is no longer there; it was washed away in a subsequent flood.

Most homes are well stocked with candles or lanterns or a gasoline-powered generator and a food supply. People don't complain much when the power goes off or the phones or Internet connections fail; it is simply a part of Mendocino life, even if it is for a few days. Then again, some people are adamant about having their own generator: the more watts, the better.

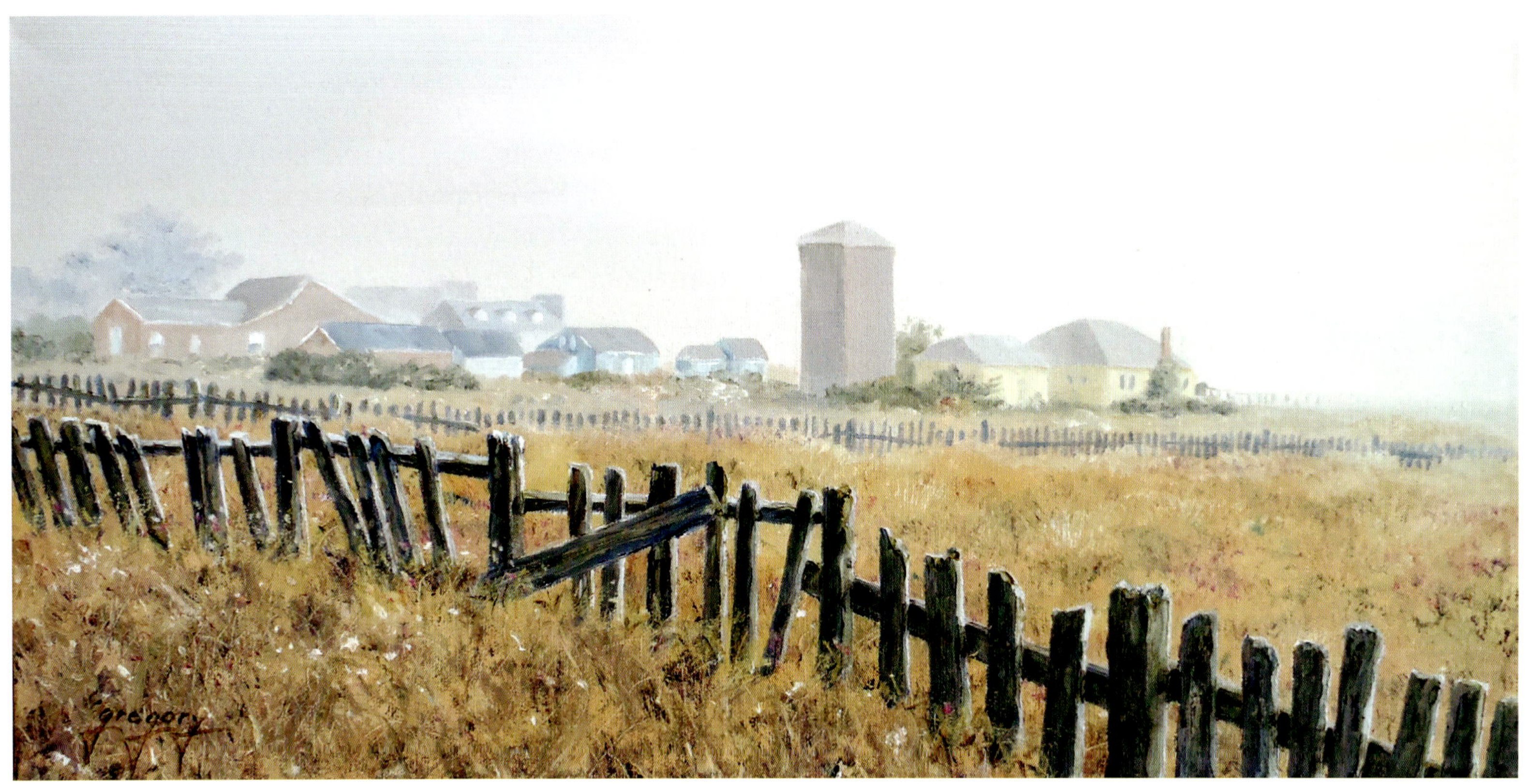

Headlands Fog, oil

Every few years Hollywood remembers that they can get that "quaint New England look" without hauling their equipment and stars all the way to the East Coast. And so, to the delight of some and the annoyance of others, we find our buildings temporarily renamed and our traffic diverted. One morning, we drove into town and discovered a forest of quite tall trees had been 'installed' overnight outside the bank (which, for the purpose of the film, had become a funeral home). The market across the street had become a bus depot. And the tourists, looking to cash a check or buy a sandwich, were confused. Among the photoplays with a Mendocino background are *East of Eden* (some locals have home movies of a sullen James Dean strolling around town); *Johnny Belinda; The Russians are Coming, The Russians are Coming; The Summer of '42, Racing With the Moon, Cujo, Dead and Buried, Karate Kid III, The Majestic,* and *Overboard.*

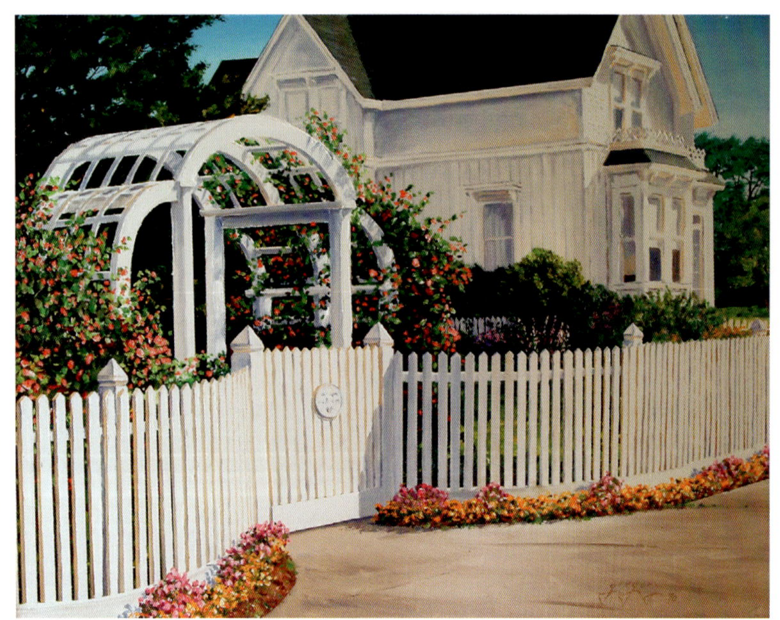

Arched Arbor, oil

As it happens, Mendocino was also the longtime residence of the last surviving cast member of *Gone With the Wind,* the late Cammie Conlon, who portrayed Rhett Butler's ill-fated daughter, Bonnie Blue Butler.

Murder, She Wrote, the popular Angela Lansbury television series was set in the fictitious town of Cabot Cove, Maine. Most of the exterior shots were filmed in Mendocino, and nine episodes took place in and around Blair House, built by Oliver Johnson in 1888 for Elisha Blair, who had come to Mendocino, appropriately enough, from Maine. More than 150 locals appeared as "background people," and the high school band also made an appearance. Blair House is now an inn.

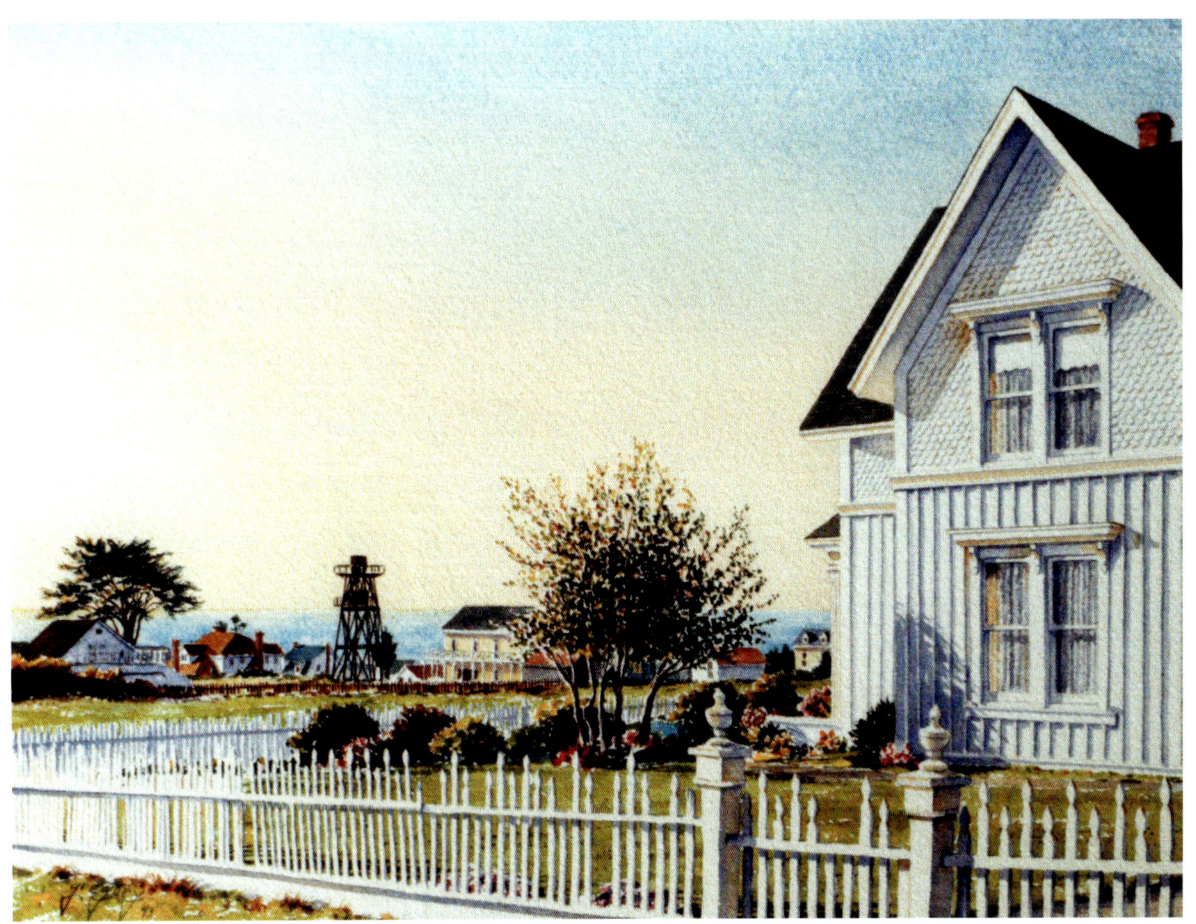

View From Blair House "Jessica's House," watercolor

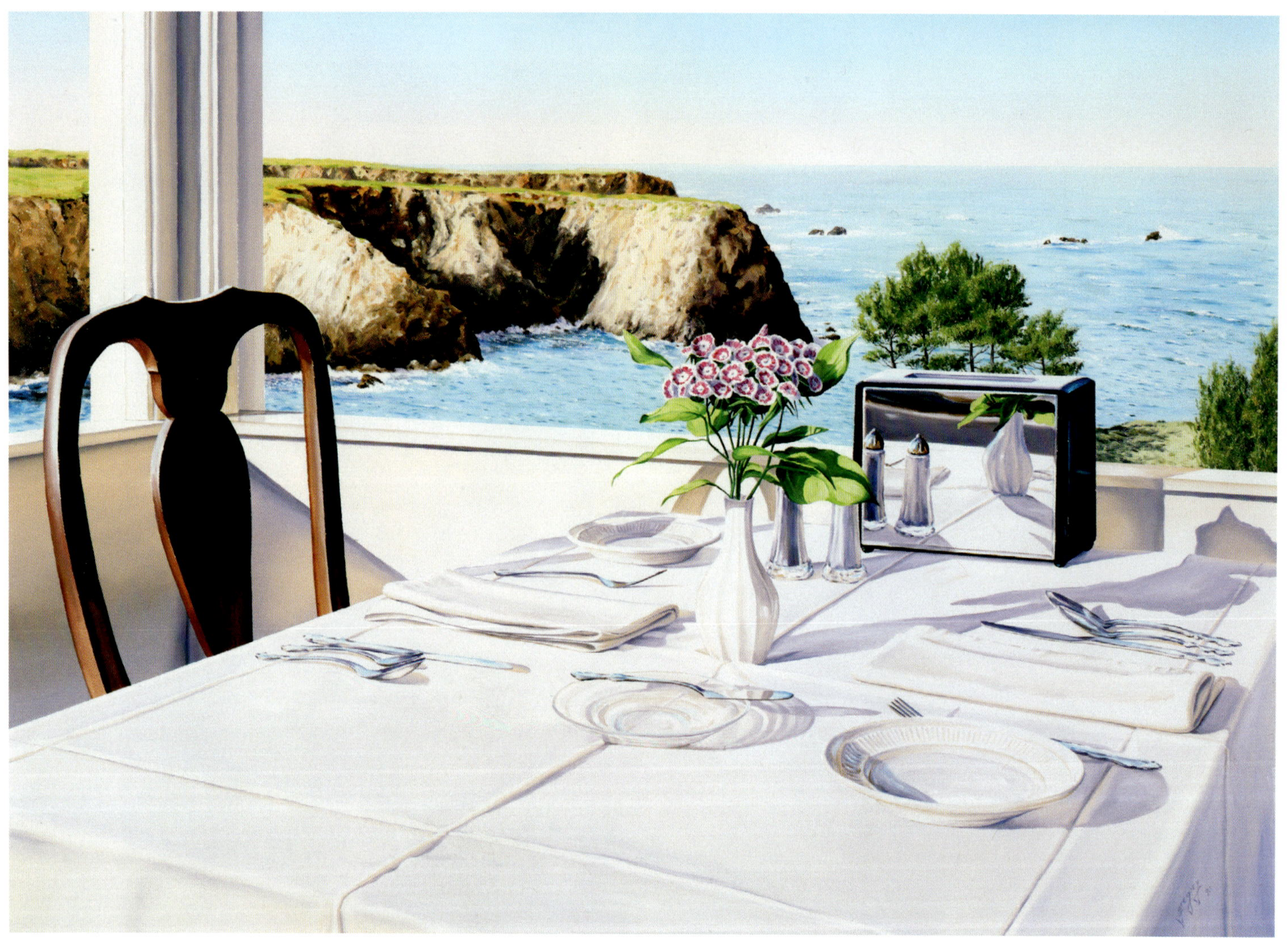

Breakfast View, oil

This is what is known in the world of computers as an "undocumented feature"— something nifty that the computer can do, which is not mentioned in the manual or the press releases, but is discovered after you buy it. Here is an excellent breakfast recipe from Mendocino's 'celebrity chef' Margaret Fox, from her book (which I helped write), *Morning Food*. Recipe © 2006, Margaret S. Fox

Mendocino Frittata

A classic frittata that allows for infinite variations

9 large eggs
2 T. minced parsley
Salt
3–4 T. olive oil
2 T. fresh thyme leaves
¼ t. cayenne pepper
¼ c. roasted garlic
½ c. cherry tomatoes, cut in half
¾ c. finely chopped red peppers
¼ c. grated dry cheese
Freshly ground pepper
⅔ c. finely chopped green onions
3 oz. goat cheese, cut into small cubes or thin slices, depending on shape
1¼ cups cubed (¾ inch) cooked peeled potatoes

- Beat eggs with parsley, dry cheese, salt, and freshly ground pepper. *Set aside.*
- Heat a large ovenproof sauté pan, add olive oil, and cook potatoes over medium heat until well browned on all sides, about 10 minutes.
- Add peppers and sauté until soft.

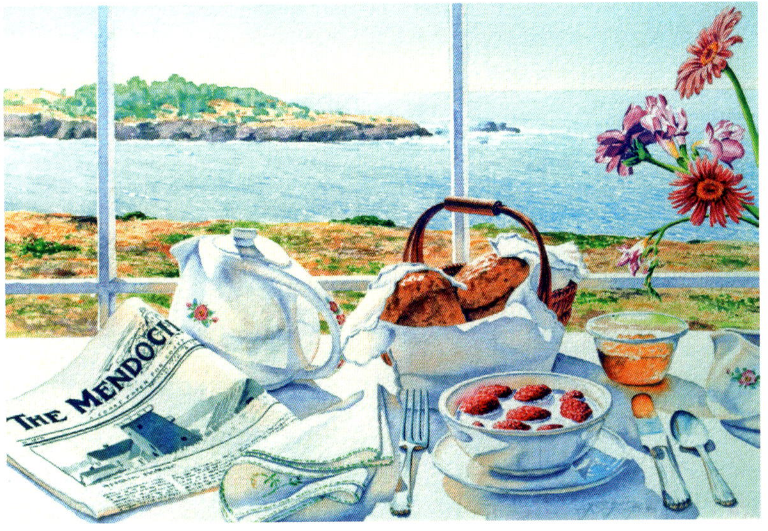

Mendocino Breakfast, watercolor

- Add green onions, cook until limp, and add thyme.
- Sprinkle cayenne pepper over vegetables and stir to distribute.
- Turn on the broiler at this point.
- Turn up the heat and add egg mixture.
- Turn heat down to medium-low. Quickly place goat cheese, cherry tomatoes and roasted garlic evenly over the surface.
- Reduce the heat to low and let cook, slowly, until the edges are set. Lift the edges so that uncooked egg can run underneath, and repeat this a couple of times during the next 5 minutes or so. Peek underneath and make sure the bottom isn't browning too quickly. If it is, reduce heat.
- When the top is set and still moist, place the pan under the broiler for 45–60 seconds, until the top is slightly browned. Slide frittata out onto a warmed dish and cut into wedges.

In 1909, Frank, patriarch of the Mendosa family, lost an arm in a mill accident. To support his wife and eight children, he opened a market, Mendosa's, one of few businesses in town to survive the closing of the mill in the early 1930s (the mill opened briefly a few years later, then shut for good) and the Great Depression, both of which were devastating to the Mendocino economy.

One bearer of the Mendosa name, following some sort of kerfuffle within the family, marched a couple of blocks down the street, and opened his own fish and meat market (the image to the right). And then the Harvest Market store in Fort Bragg acquired the original Mendosa's, having the good sense to keep the name on the sign, now as "Harvest at Mendosas."

With regard to new businesses, more than a few city people harbor the fantasy that one day they will sell everything, move to a beautiful place, and put their business, managerial, cooking, manufacturing or entrepreneurial skills to work by starting a small business. One common problem is that most tourists come to Mendocino during the tourist season, and their business musings are beguiled by seeing crowds on the streets, lines waiting to get into restaurants, and "no vacancy" signs in profusion on the doors of bed and breakfast inns. These people should be required by law to spend a week in Mendocino during a cold January rainstorm before signing any contracts or checks.

When such people ask, "What do you need or want here?" the answer is often in the direction of something as much for the locals as the visitors. At various times, the answer has been a drug store, a shoe store, a toy store, a clothing store, but not, please, another gallery, boutique or tee shirt shop.

Or psychic reader. Once, I moved out of my local office on Main Street, but there was still a month to go on the lease. Indulging a silly fantasy, I applied to the Historical Review Board to put up a discreet sign for a month reading, "John Bear, Ph.D., Crystal Ball Reading." Following a spirited hearing, the permit was granted and the chairman added, "But of course you knew that would happen." I opened for business one Saturday morning, but was so dispirited by the desperate people who came in looking for personal advice that I closed up three hours later. I should have anticipated that, eh?

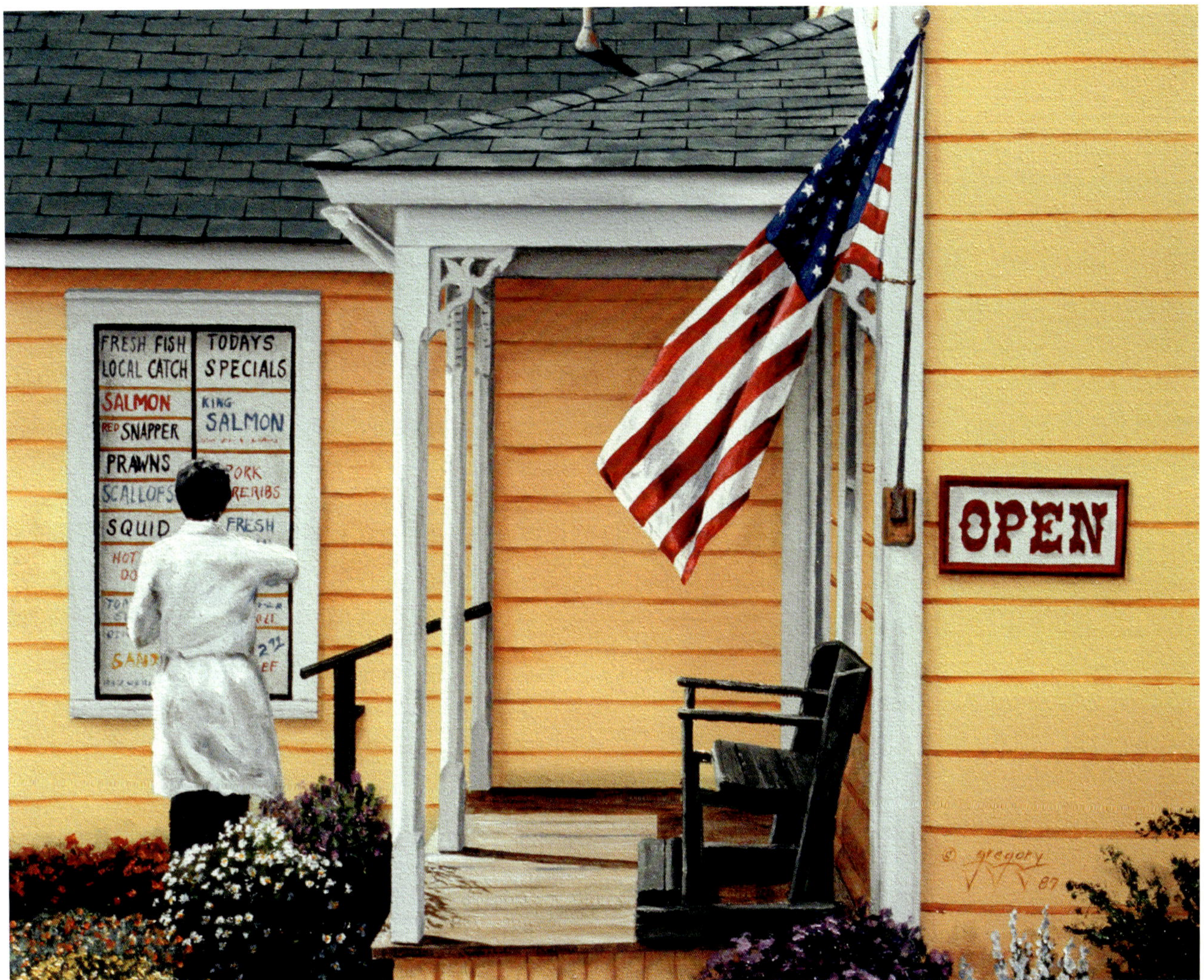

Today's Catch, oil

Kelley Pond, situated just off Main Street near Kelley House, is either the place to see the wild calla lilies, some rather aggressive geese and a lovely reflected view of MacCallum House, or it is the place to discover that Mendocino is having another of its perennial water shortages, whereupon the pond will contain little or nothing in the way of water and few, if any, geese.

There is no public water system in Mendocino; people depend on their own wells, on the kindness of neighbors, and sometimes on the entrepreneurs with good inland wells and tank trucks. Some claim the water shortage is due to over development and construction. Others suggest that wells have been erratic in Mendocino for 160 years.

Most city people never give a thought to their water: it is what comes out of the faucet when you turn the valve. But in Mendocino it is a precious commodity. The first attempt at a well on our land, a hand-dug affair, came up dry, leaving us with a hole in the ground three feet wide and sixty feet deep. Thinking that some day we'd find a use for such a 'hidey hole,' we simply covered it over, where it it still presumably sits beneath the front porch of an unsuspecting homeowner. The next well attempt on our land was drilled at the height of a long drought. The engineer came out with his geological maps, his soil test kits, and his assorted scientific instruments. After a bit he said, "I think I will drill right here–but first let me check it with my divining rod." We didn't ask questions; we were just grateful that a plentiful supply was found at a depth of 150 feet.

The "Kelley" of Kelley House, William Kelly, came west from Prince Edward Island, Canada seeking gold, but in Mendocino (where he arrived in 1852 as a ship's carpenter), he found cheap timber and cheaper land. (The second "e" in his surname didn't arrive in Mendocino until much later.)

Kelly bought most of the Mendocino peninsula, and a few years later sold 200 acres at $30 an acre to the newly-arrived William Heeser. Heeser in turn carved some of the land into one-fourteenth of an acre parcels, and sold them at $40 each (the equivalent of $560 an acre) to local workingmen, presumably the start of the real estate industry in Mendocino.

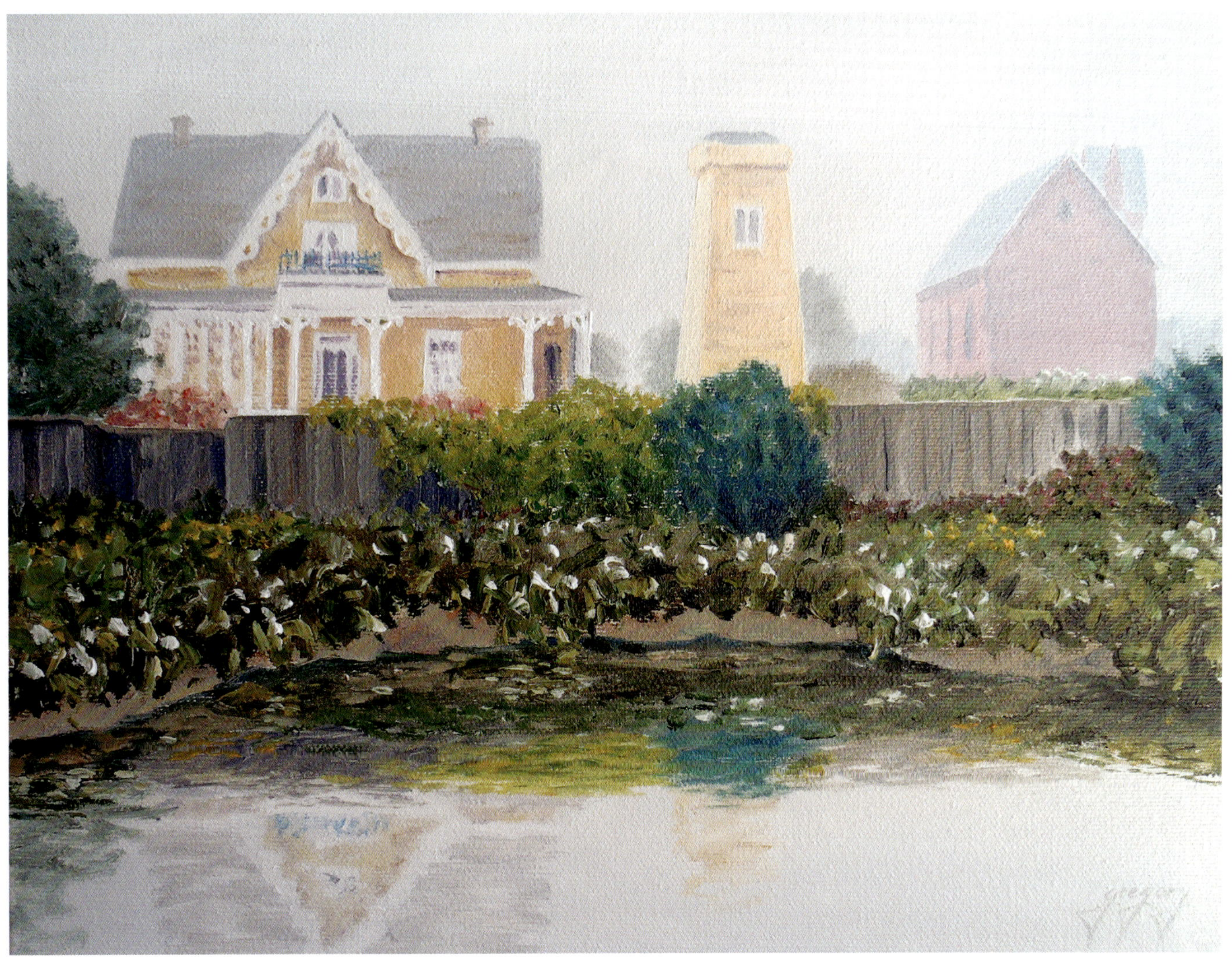

Kelley Pond, oil

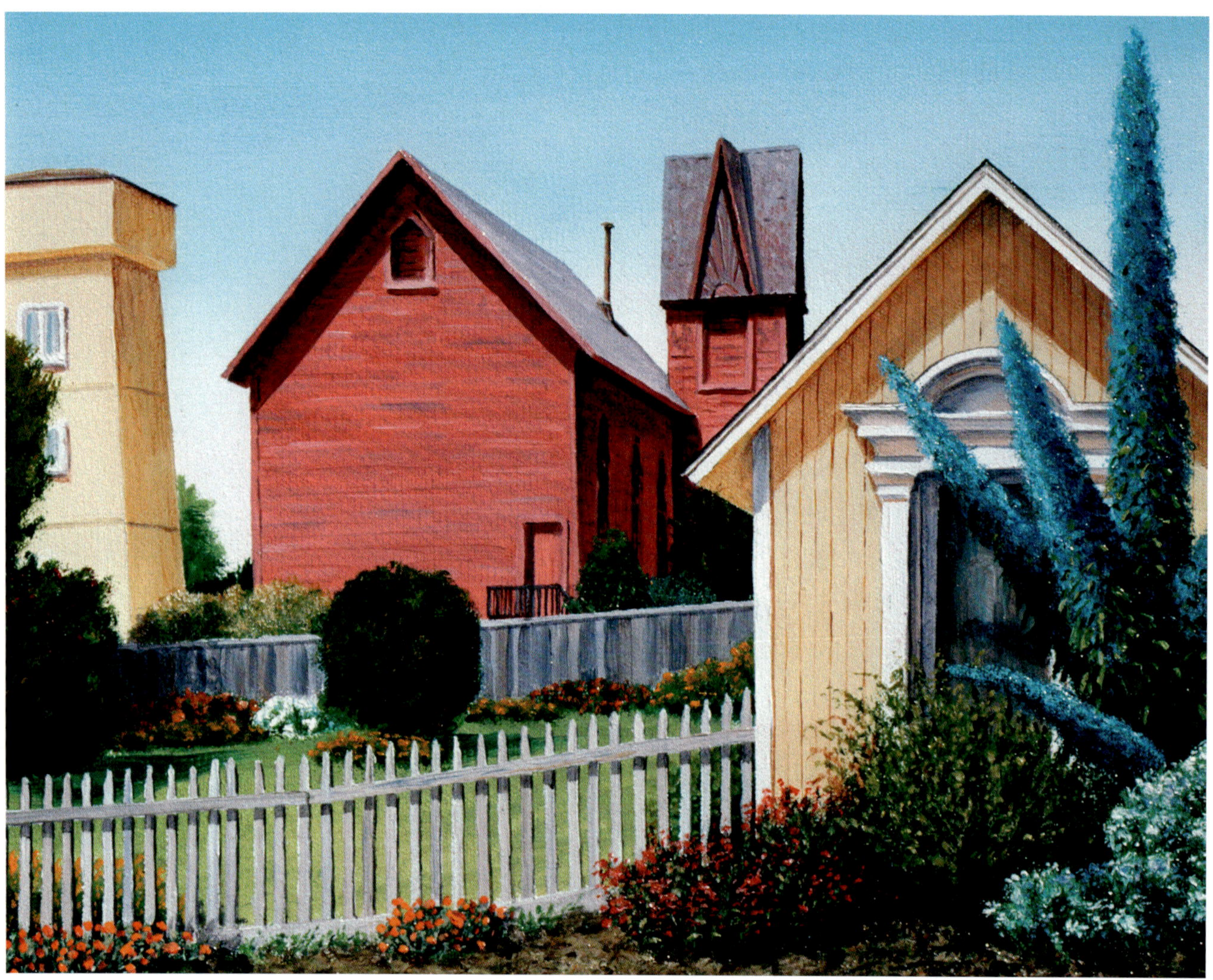

Eliza's Old Red Church, oil

Eliza Lee Kelly was the wife of William Kelly, one of the founders of Mendocino, and mother of Daisy MacCallum. She was a Baptist, and there were not many of those in Mendocino in the early days. As the population grew, Eliza asked her husband to build her a church. What is still known as "Eliza's Old Red Church" was dedicated in 1894, the year before William Kelly's death.

Eliza invited a fellow Canadian, the Rev. John Ross of Caspar, to serve in her church. Reverend Ross was a traveling preacher, calling on Baptists along 100 miles of coastline, from Westport to Point Arena. In the Rev. Ross's absence, Eliza preached some sermons herself. The church was in use until Eliza's death in 1914.

After a long hiatus, the old red church again returned to community service, this time as a natural food collective. (The Baptists had built a new church nearby.) The food collective caused some eyebrows to raise ("Socialism right here in Mendocino?") but most people were pleased to find a wide range of natural and organic products. And Corners of the Mouth has thrived for decades, still collectively owned.

William Heeser bought a great deal of land in town from William Kelly, and in 1877 started a newspaper, the *Beacon*, which remained in the Heeser family for 99 years, when the last individual owner, a cousin by marriage, sold it to a Southern California chain of newspapers.

For many in Mendocino, it was as if an old friend—one you kind of took for granted—had suddenly died. The anguish was compounded when the new owners destroyed the old photographic plates, junked the old but functional printing equipment, and replaced the editor. The concern crossed all boundaries of age and politics. Meetings were held to discuss starting a new paper or buying back the *Beacon,* attended by members of the John Birch Society, the I.W.W. (then alive and well on the coast) and people of all viewpoints in between.

Finally, the new owner of the paper flew in to assure us that nothing would be changed. With the passage of time, high dudgeon turned to low dudgeon and eventually no dudgeon at all. And when the Southern California chain subsequently sold "our" *Beacon* to an Arkansas publishing conglomerate, most people hardly noticed.

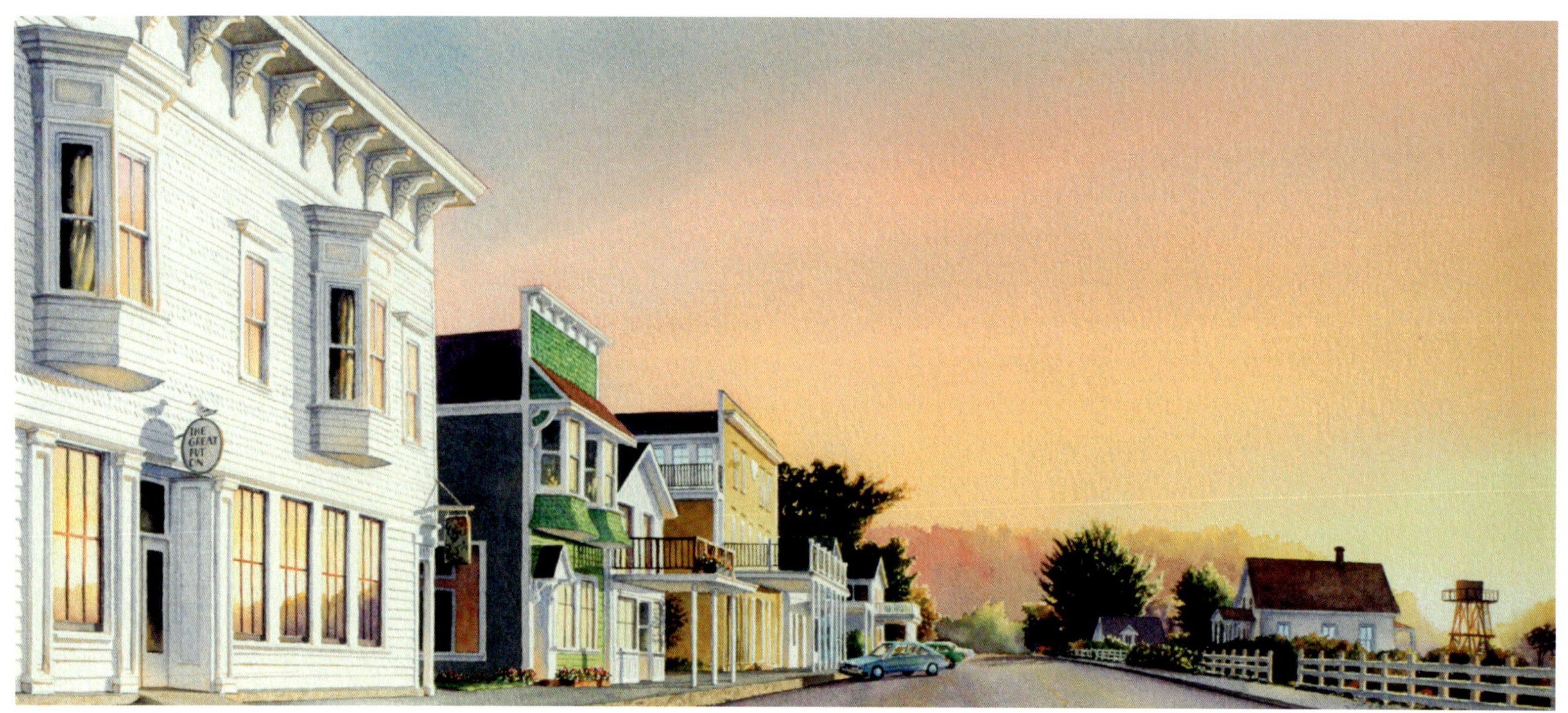

Main Street Sunrise, watercolor

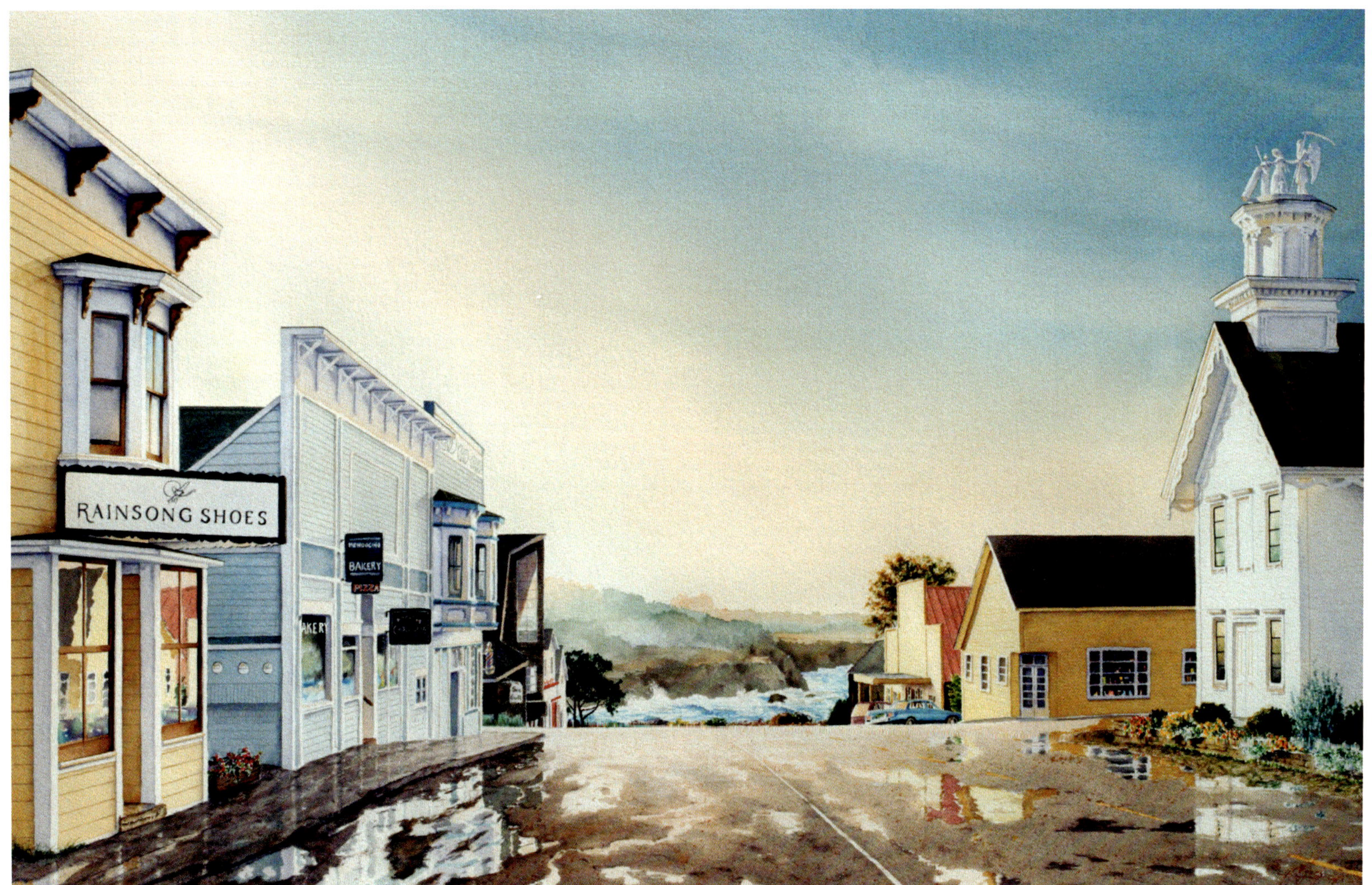

Rainsong, oil

Some of the loveliest land in Mendocino is given over to the cemeteries. There are cemeteries for Catholics, for Protestants, for Jews, for the Chinese, and for others. The biggest is Hillcrest Cemetery, home to about a thousand souls, from (alphabetically) Charlotte Abernethy to Billy Zissa. Although there has been a Chinese cemetery since 1863, the Chinese residents of Mendocino were isolated from the community in death as they were in life, and many older Chinese went home to China to die. If they died in Mendocino, their remains were shipped to China for burial.

The Chinese were a major presence in northern California in the years following the discovery of gold. Many came to seek their fortunes in the gold fields and stayed to work as cooks and laborers in the mines and the mills, or to build the railroads. Some opened shops and laundries; some went into farming. But they rarely became a part of the community, whether by their choice or by an anti-Chinese sentiment among the old timers. By the 1860s, Mendocino was home to more than 500 Chinese, including dozens of children, but the children were not welcome in the public schools. Finally a private tuition-supported one-room Chinese school was established in 1889 which, as the Mendocino *Beacon* reported, "solves the vexed question of admitting Chinese children into our public school, over which there has been considerable trouble here."

Mendocino is the site of one of only three Joss houses, or Chinese temples, remaining in California. It was built in the 1850s by a group including "Joe" Lee, whose junk sailed from China and put ashore just north of Mendocino. In 1995, Lee's descendants, the last Chinese family in Mendocino, deeded the Temple property to a new non-profit organization. It was restored and painted, and rededicated in 2001 in a ceremony involving lion dancers and nuns from the City of Ten Thousand Buddhas in Ukiah.

My dear mother-in-law, Mary Dorrow, is buried here, in an inadvertantly-unmarked grave. At the time of her burial, we decided to add a marker or "tombstone" later, and "later" became twenty years. By the time we were ready, no one seemed to know just where to find her. We're still working on this issue.

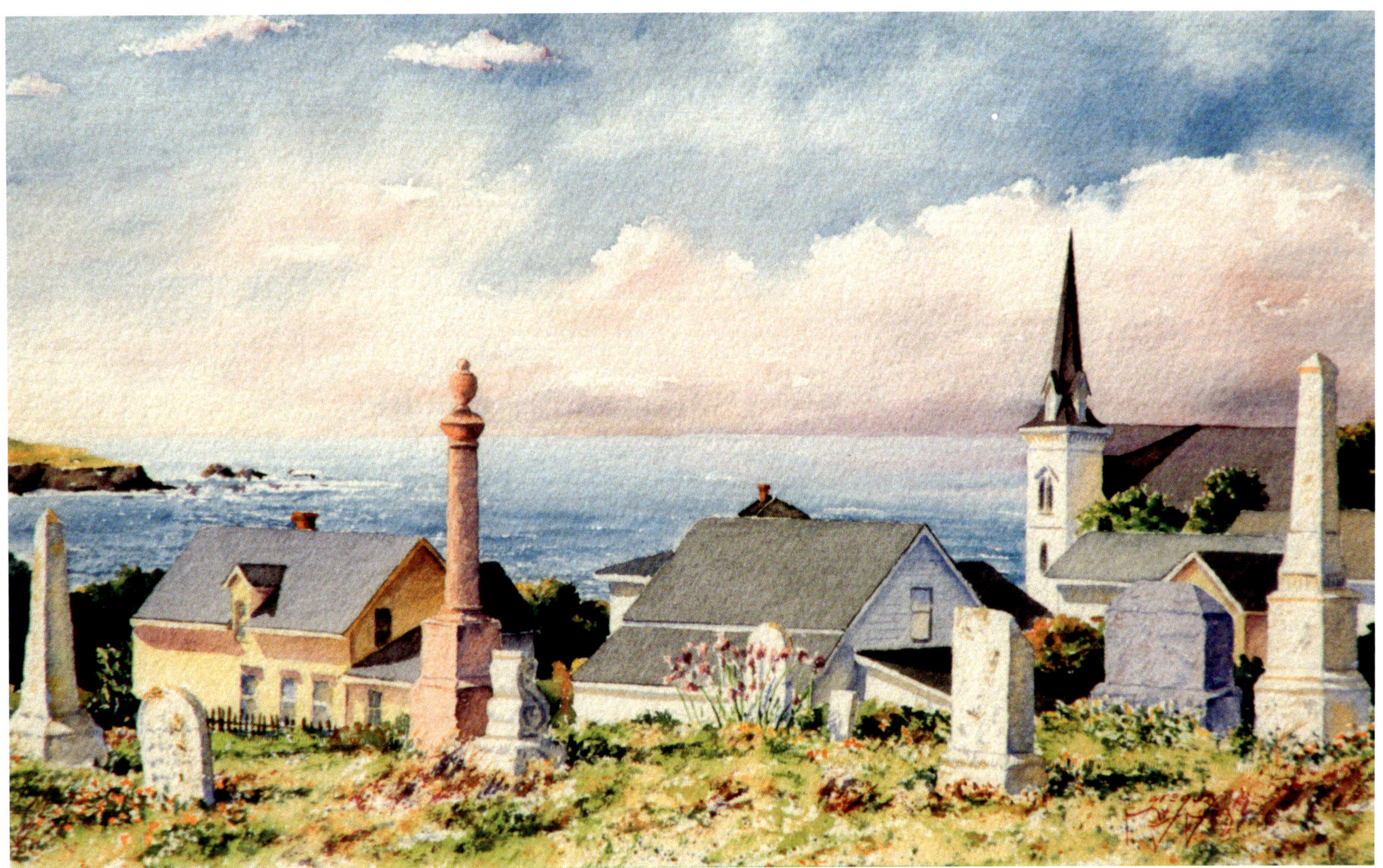

Evergreen Cemetery, watercolor

Consider the image of Daisy MacCallum, born in Mendocino in 1859, and living with her aging son in the house that was her wedding present, well into her nineties, 43 years a widow, rocking back and forth on her porch, perhaps watching the fishing boats that sometimes come south from Noyo Harbor into Mendocino Bay, or smiling at the whale that, on rare occasions, will leave its northbound pod to frolic for a short while off the headlands.

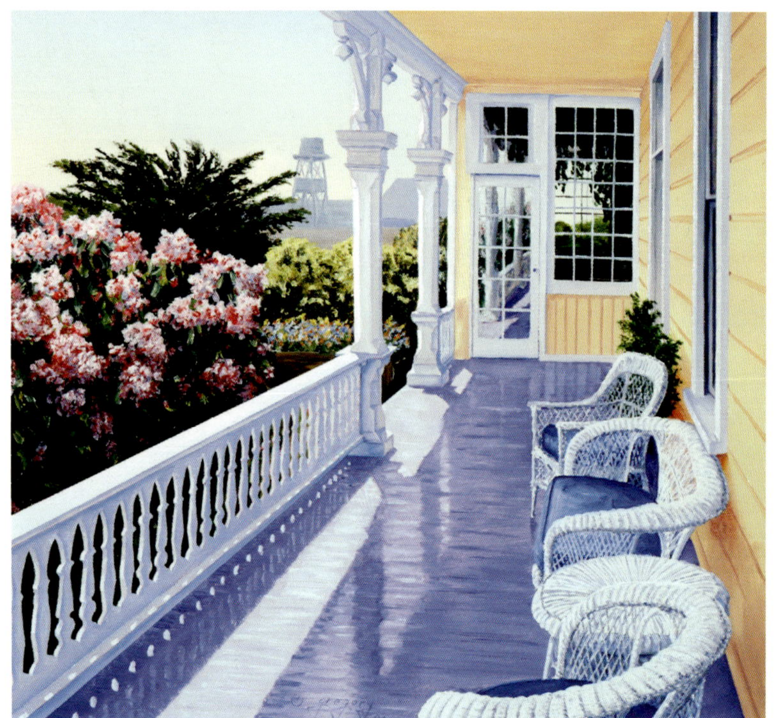

Wicker, oil

Contemplate the lifespan of this woman and the changes she saw. She was born the year before Lincoln was first elected president and the only way to reach Mendocino was by sailing ship up the coast; even the first stage coaches were quite a way off. Her adventurous life included being in San Francisco at the time of the 1906 earthquake and, at 65, in Egypt for the opening of King Tut's tomb. She died as US and Russian jets were engaged in dogfights in the sky over Korea.

MacCallum House is now an inn. And in the kind of transition that seems so appropriate for Mendocino, in 2002, MacCallum House was taken over by three Mendocino natives, Megan and Jed Ayres and Noah Sheppard, two of whom had worked there part-time while attending Mendocino High School. (A local, reading a draft of this book, said, "Tell them to put more vegetarian and fish dishes on the menu." Done.)

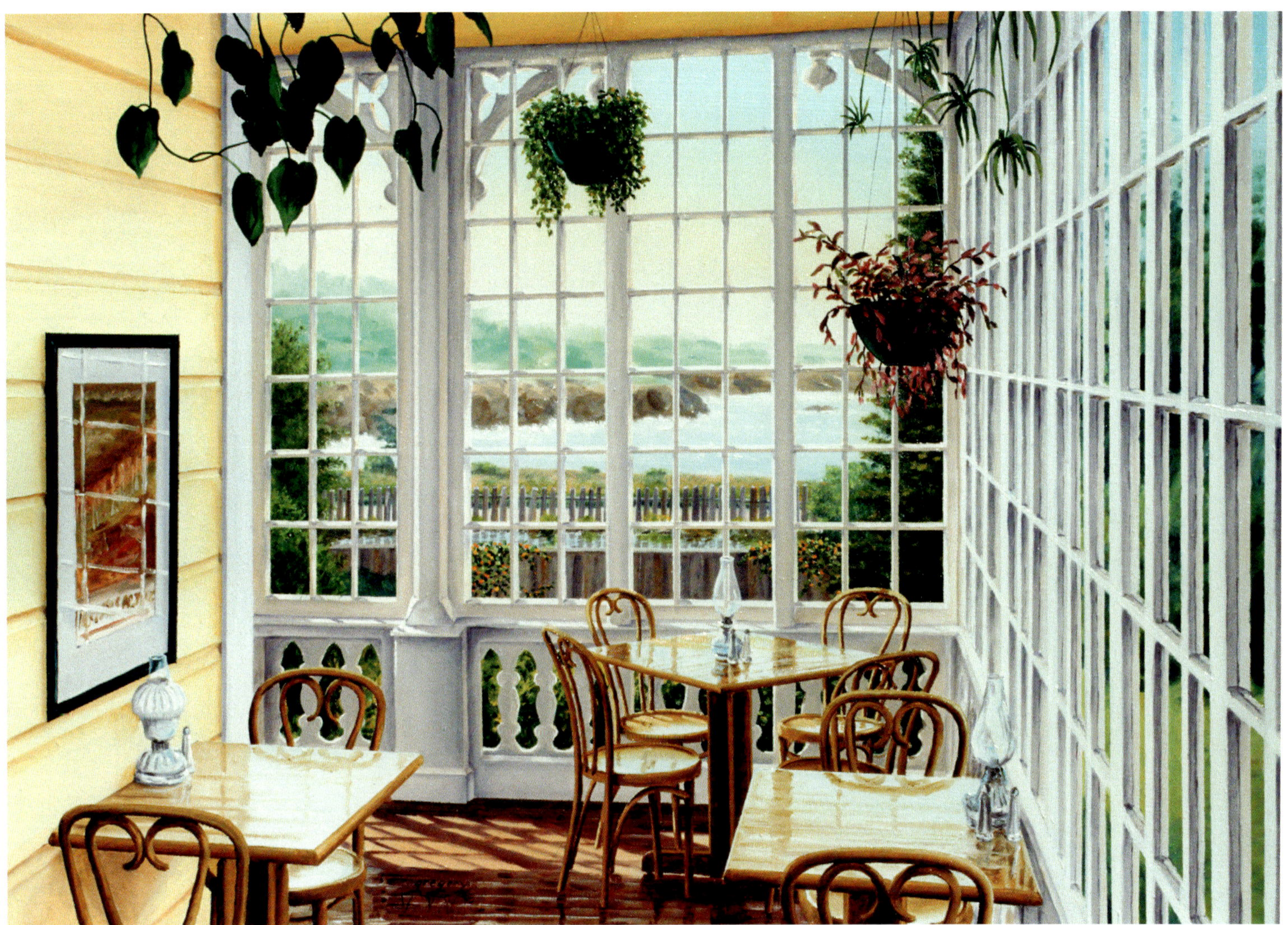

***MacCallum House Sun Porch*, oil**

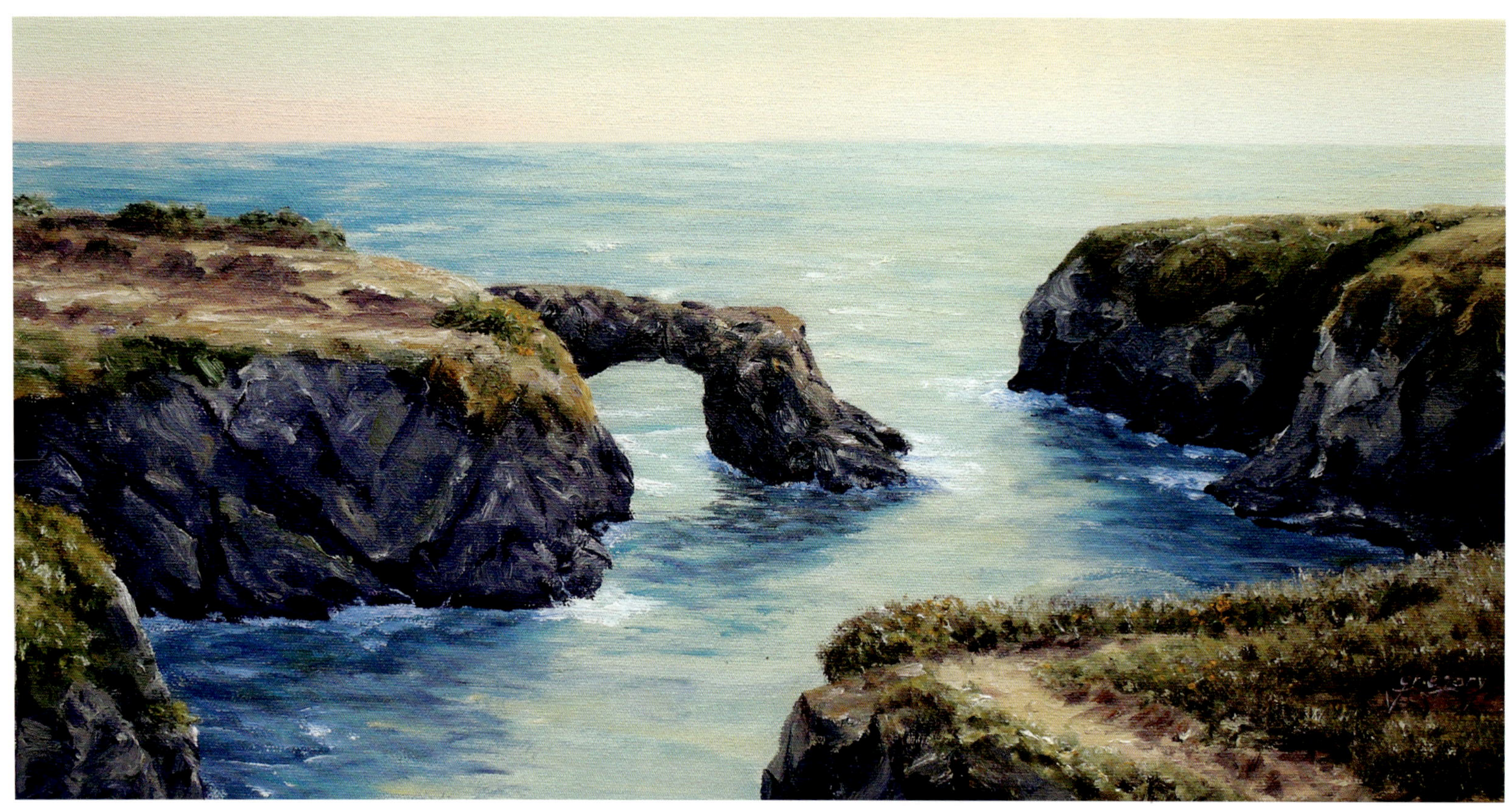

Sea Arch, oil

The Mendocino headlands are beautiful, and they are treacherous—all the more dangerous because they often appear so calm and peaceful. Just as approximately one wave out of nine is larger than those that have come before, so too is one wave every few months a killer: huge and unexpected, roaring out of a relatively calm sea. When one of those hits, inevitably people somewhere along the coast are swept away. The often repeated advice, "Don't turn your back on the ocean" is not just a slogan; it is literally a way of life.

Spectacular oceanfront surrounds Mendocino on three sides, but unexpectedly, there are no oceanfront homes. There might have been but for two people. August Heeser donated much of the headlands for a state park in honor of his father. And prominent artist Emmy Lou Packard led the fight to save the rest, when Boise Cascade wanted to build a residential development on the headlands. The Mendocino Land Trust owns the land on the ocean side of downtown, with the best views of water and town. Thankfully, the trails, paths, and bluffs are now secure for hikers, joggers, hand-in-hand strollers, and more than a few contemplatives, each with a favorite place to sit.

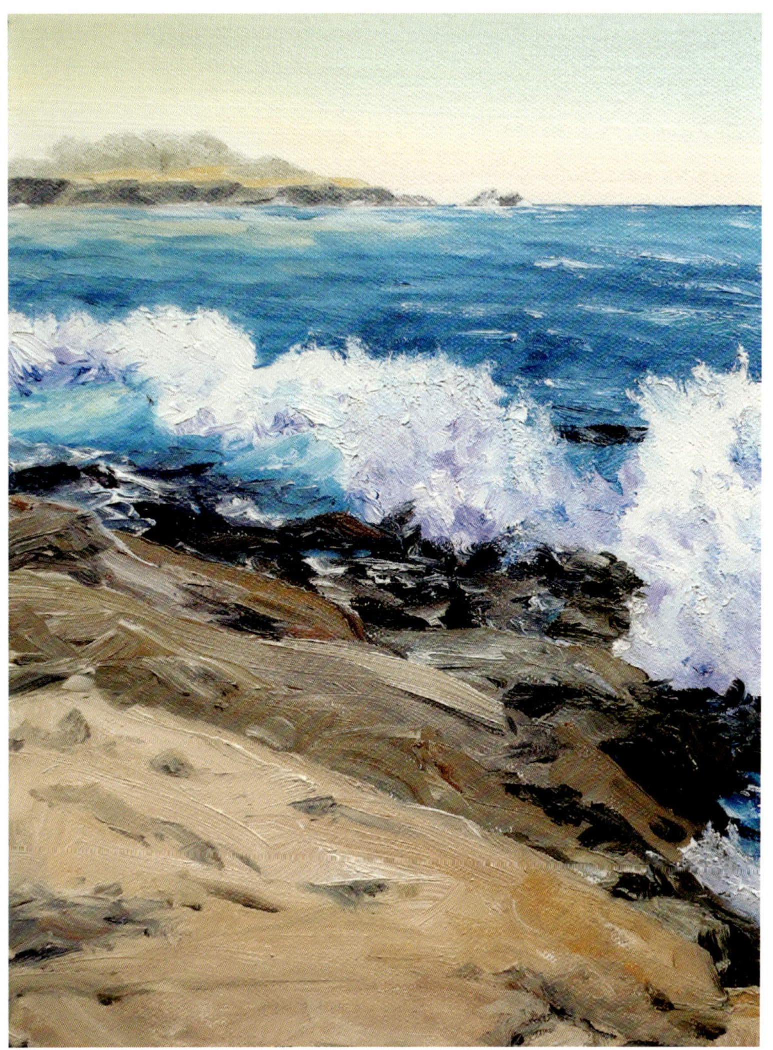

Breaking Wave, oil

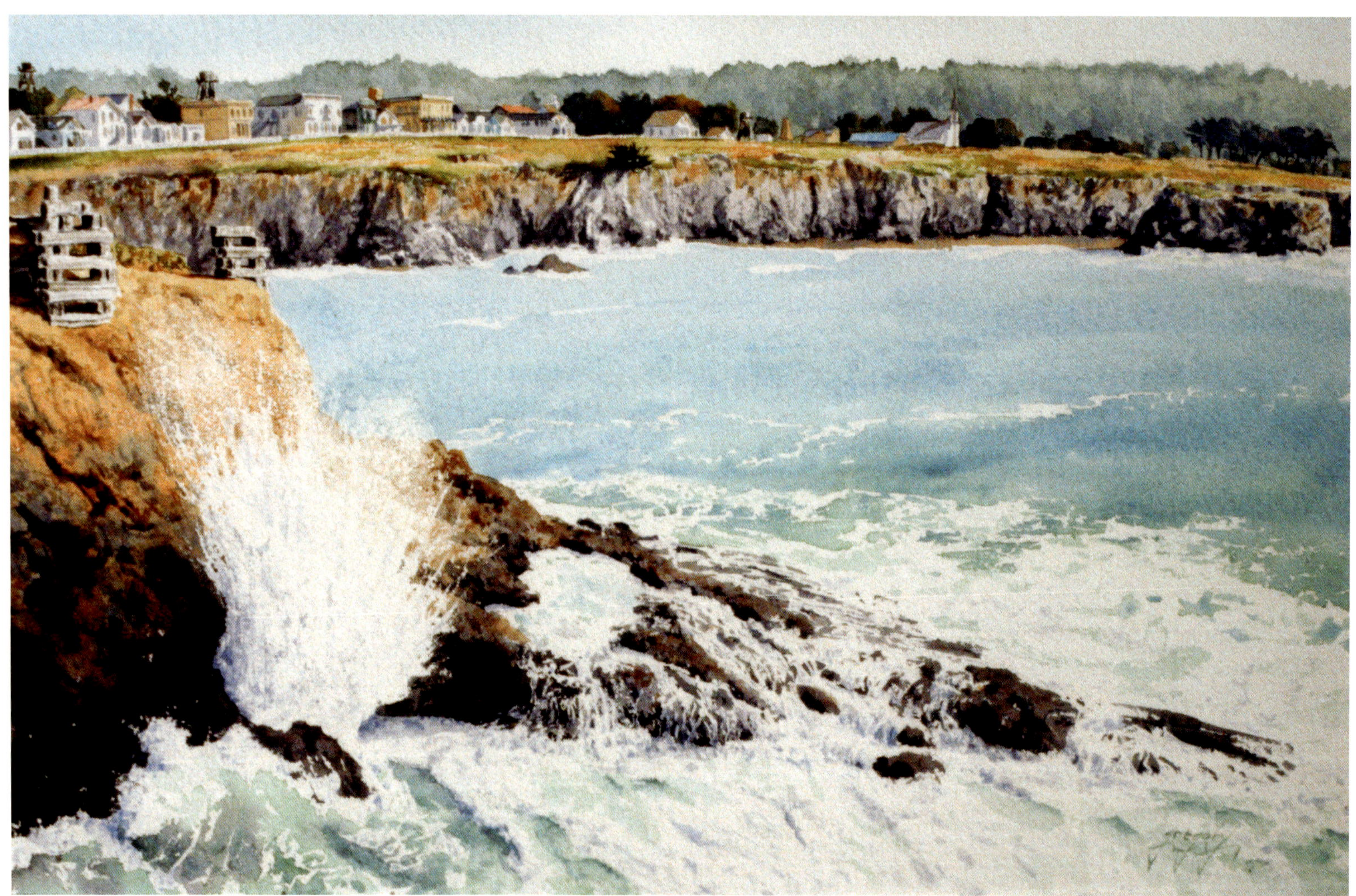

Blowhole, watercolor

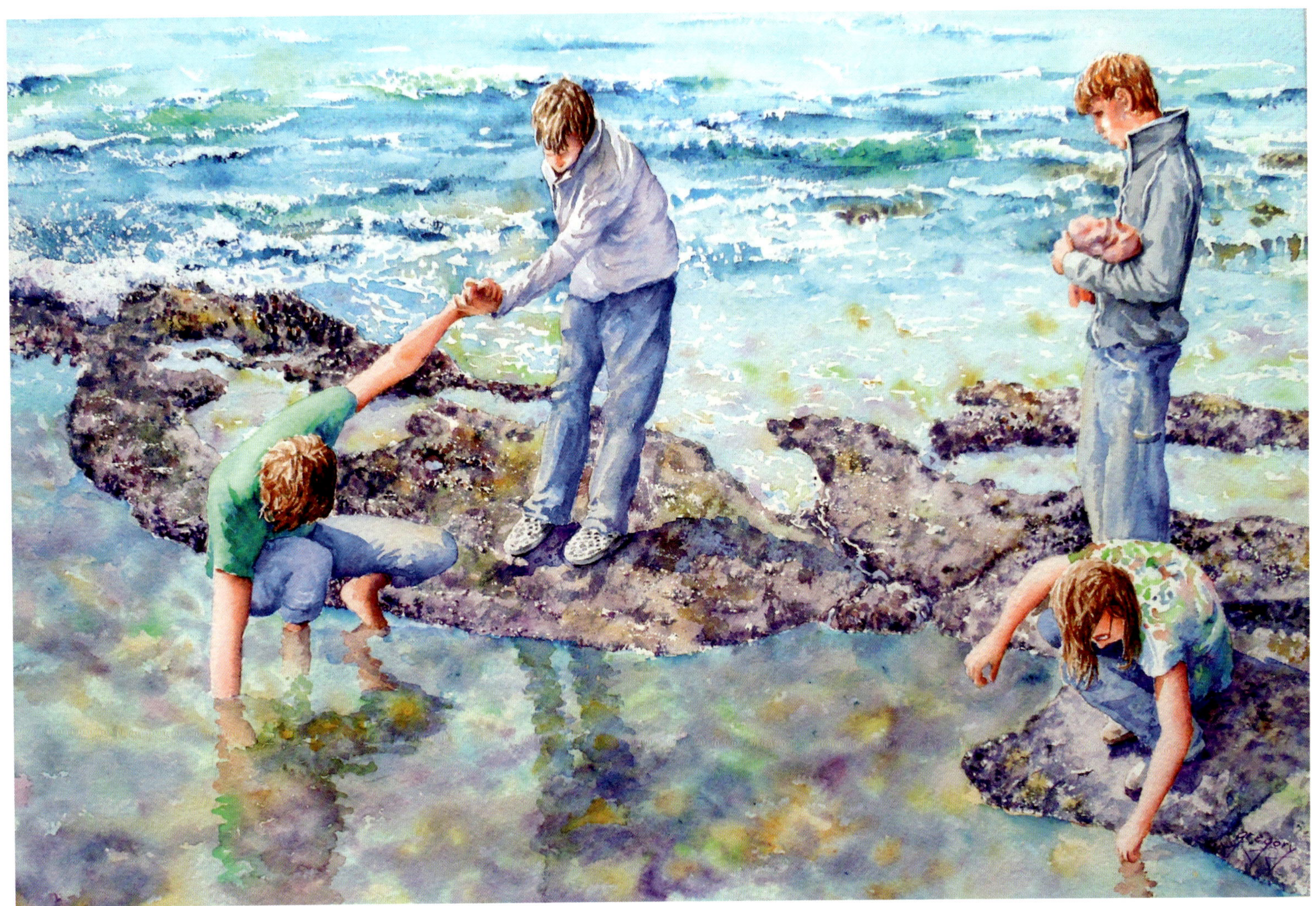

Tide Pools, watercolor

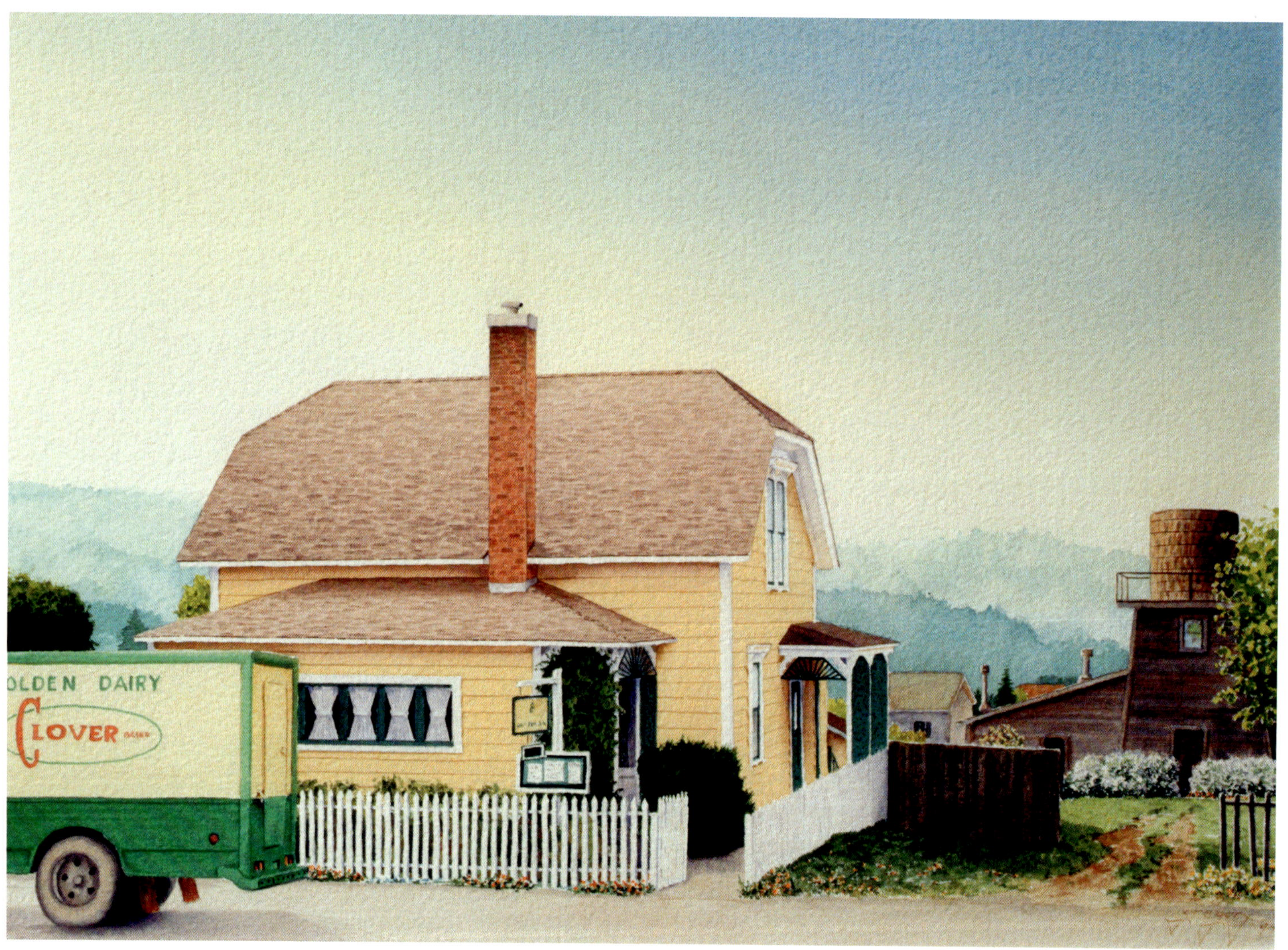

Cafe Beaujolais, watercolor

Margaret Fox came to Mendocino shortly after she earned her Bachelor's degree in psychology, bought the 36-seat Cafe Beaujolais restaurant, and worked very hard for 23 years building its clientele and reputation into what an influential critic, Ruth Reichl, called the best breakfasts in California, before selling it in 2000.[1]

Margaret believes there is always a living to be made in Mendocino by creative people willing to work really hard. "Would you rather live in the city, breathe smog, triple lock your door every night, and make a lot of money; or live in Mendocino, breathe air, rarely lock anything, and make a good deal less? There are no simple answers, and the only foolish answers are those that are made in haste without considering all the ramifications."

1 Full and happy disclosure: Margaret and I collaborated on two books: *Cafe Beaujolais* (what it is like to run a small rural restaurant, plus many recipes), and *Morning Food*, which gives permission to eat whatever we want in the morning, and provides lots of unusual recipes to make it happen. The former is hard to find but may be redone; the latter is revised and updated from the Ten Speed Press division of Random House.

With the mysterious exception of gasoline, typically significantly less than the Bay Area, prices tend to be higher in the Mendocino area. It is increasingly expensive to ship goods into and out of town. And so coastal residents are faced with prospect of paying higher prices or filling up the SUV at the discount stores in Santa Rosa, thereby ignoring the important 3/50 project and helping to doom local businesses.

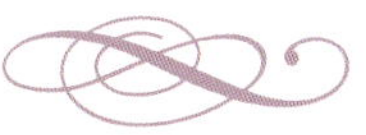

3/50 project? A most admirable idea, described on local posters, pointing out that if everyone would make just three purchases of $50 at local stores they didn't want to lose, instead of in the big city or on the Internet, it would go a long way to helping local businesses survive. That would be three purchases per month, or per year, or per lifetime; anything helps. (So if you would like to buy another copy or two of this very book, please consider doing so at one of the bookshops in Mendocino or Fort Bragg. Thank you.)

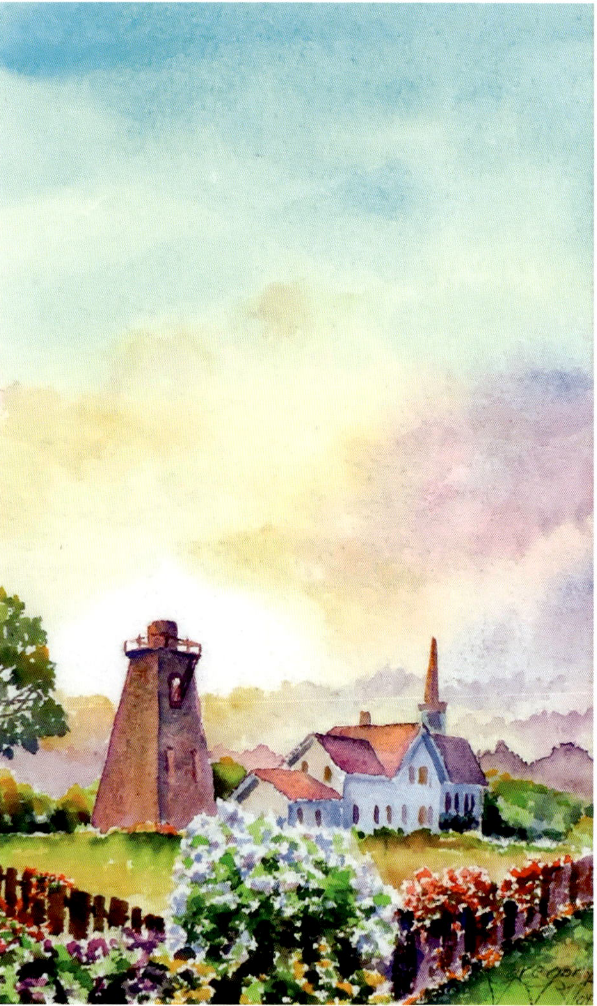

Morning Sky, watercolor

Mendocino does not offer much in the way of white-collar employment. And yet it has great appeal to white collar people, many of whom are more than willing to make a rather dramatic career (and collar color) change in order to survive in the country.

And so, among many others, one finds, in and around Mendocino, a former stockbroker who sweeps chimneys, a former computer executive who repairs sewing machines; a former NASA official who is a plumber, a former college professor who sells candy, a former publishing executive who drives a bus, and a former naval officer who manufactures ice cream. How many of them would return to their old jobs? Do you see any hands raised?

During one of the recurring battles over whether the proposed remodeling of an old building was "historically accurate" or not, a frustrated landlord complained, "If they really want this town to be historically accurate, they should issue licenses to operate a dozen brothels up and down Main Street."

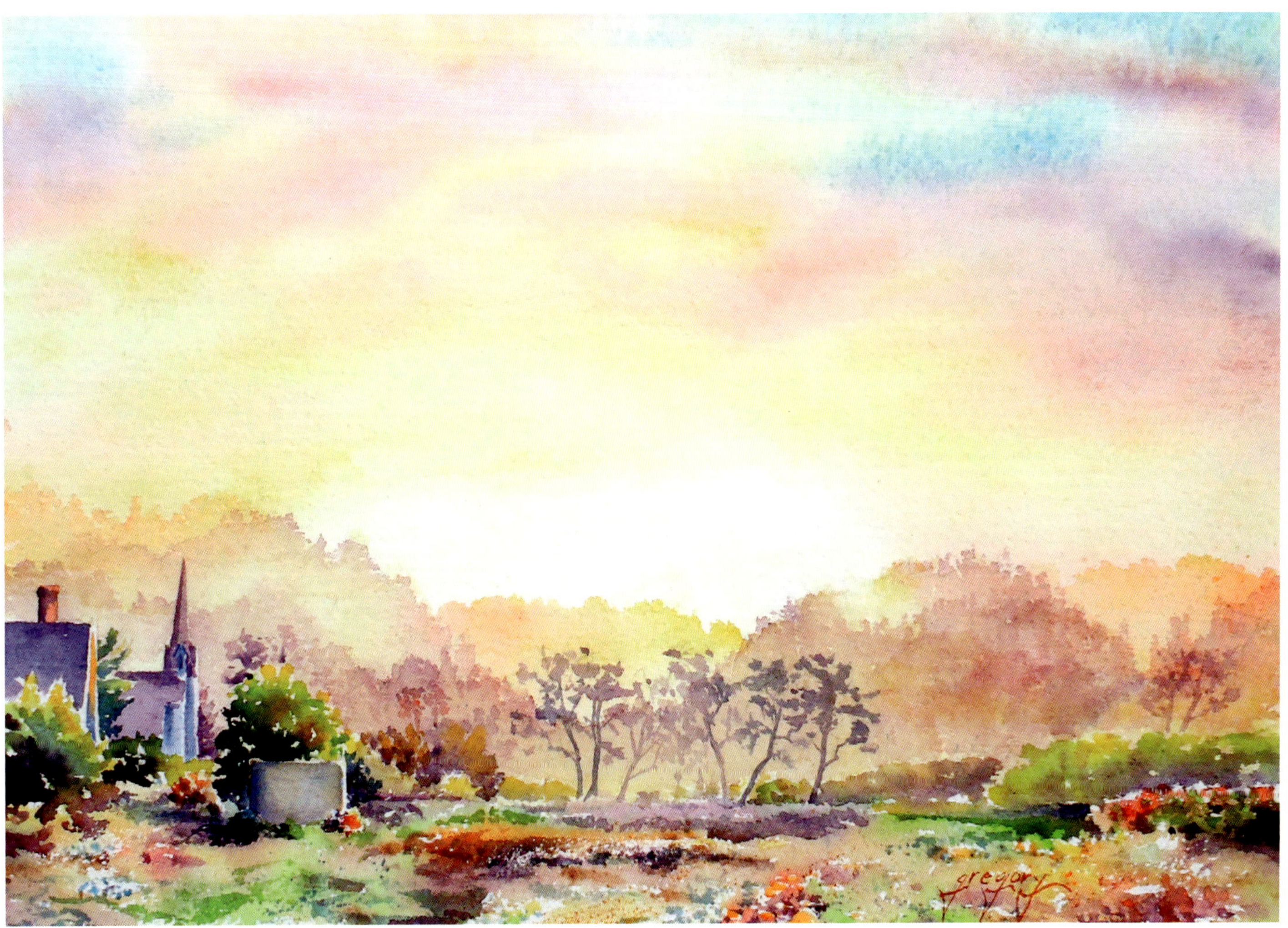

Headlands Sunrise, watercolor

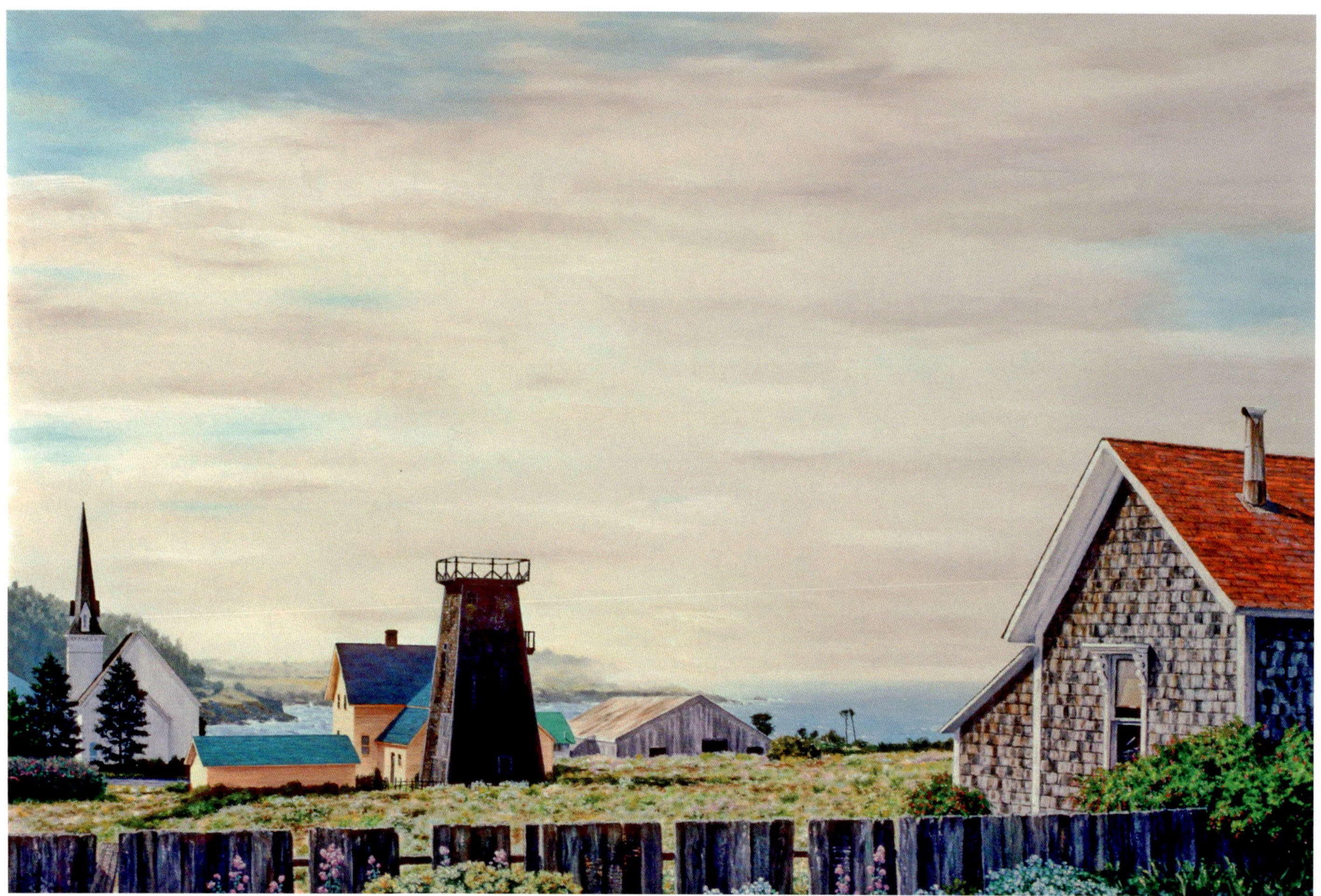

Mendocino Morning, oil

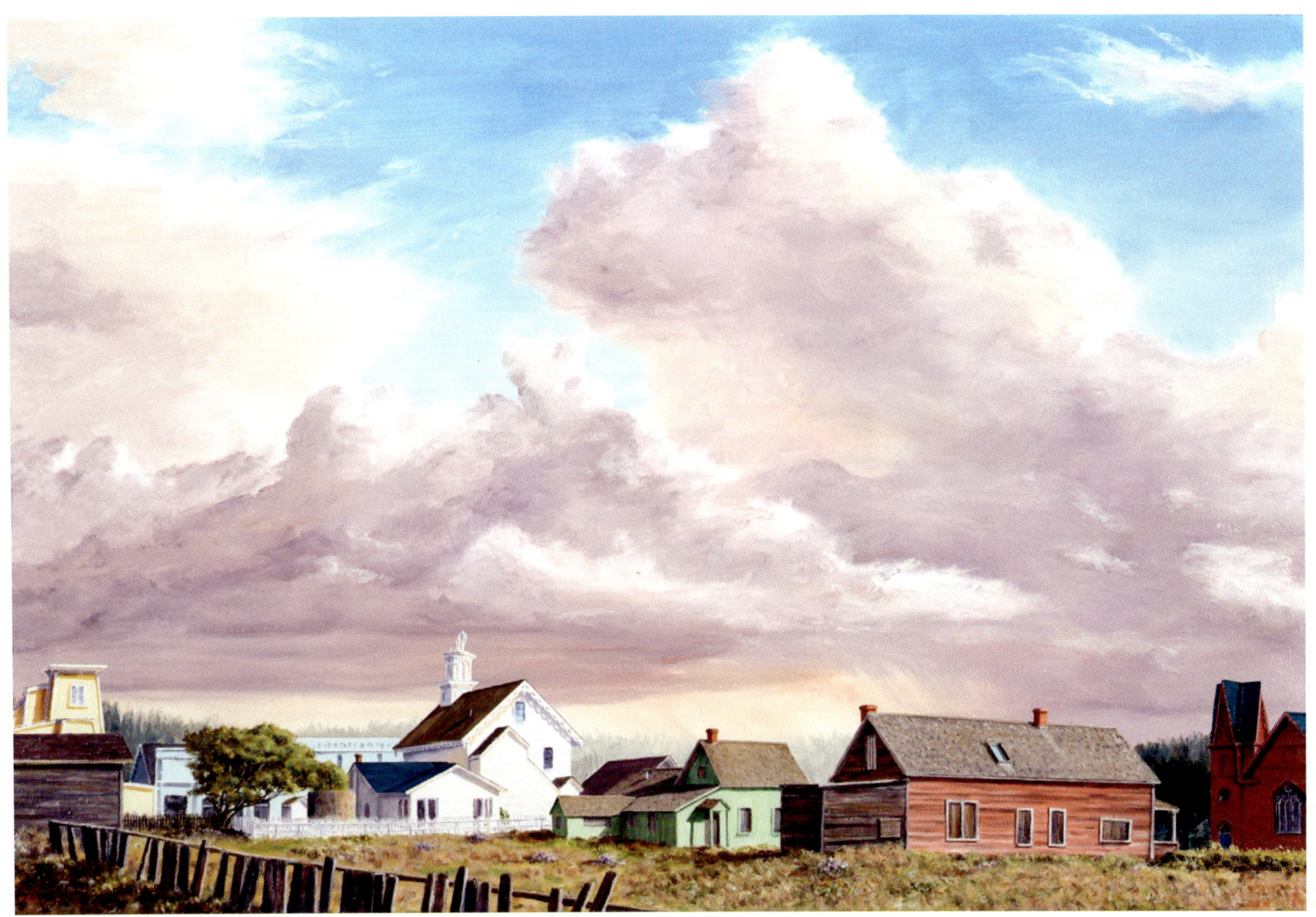

Storm Clouds Over Mendocino, oil

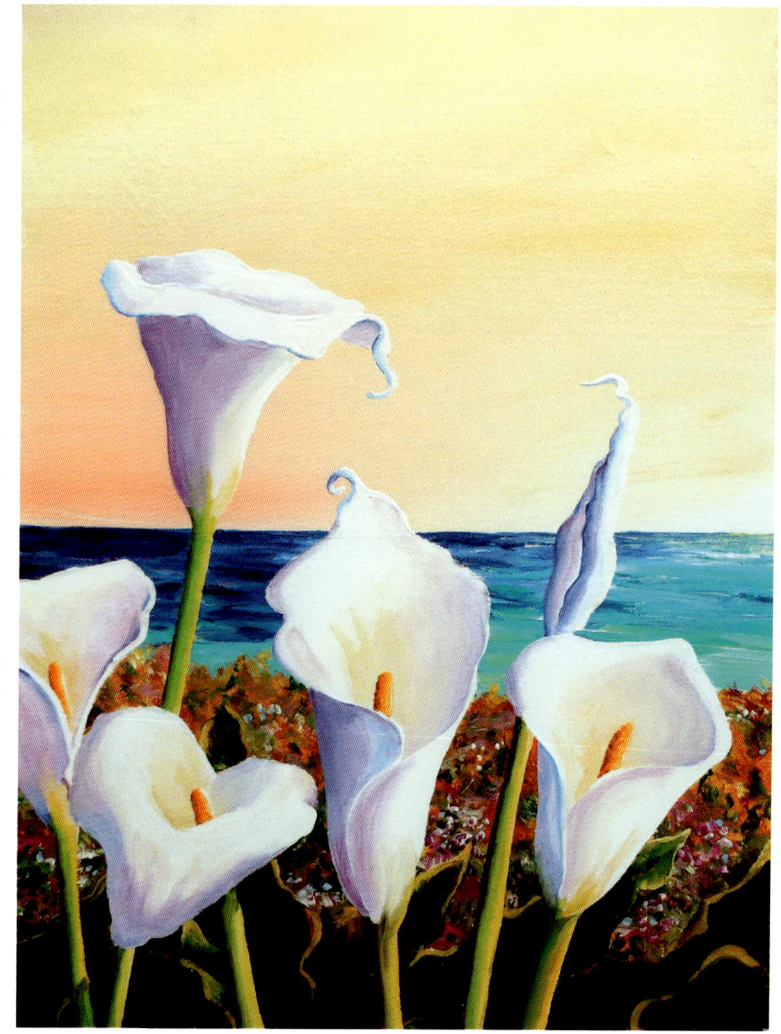

Sunset Lilies, oil

The generally cool, often damp climate along the coast is not conducive to the intentional growing of many agricultural commodities other than rhododendrons and fuchsias. But Mother Nature seems to do just fine with "volunteer" plants: calla lilies, and especially with her Scotch broom, which for a time seemed bent on overrunning much of the roadside between Mendocino and Caspar to the north.

The *zantedschia aethiopica* shown here, is a perennial, which behaves as an evergreen when the climate is damp and rainy, and a deciduous plant in dryer times. In Mendocino, it gets to do both, thriving in the winter and spring, and hanging on in the summer and fall. In other words, if you've lost your calendar, you can tell the season by inspecting the calla lilies of Mendocino.

One year, we made a deal with a local farmer: he would till three acres of our coastal land, we would plant rye grass and fava beans, and all of us would share in the proceeds of the harvest. Well, the rye was sparse, the beans rotted in the ground, the tractor broke down, and the farmer had a heart attack. We probably should have gone into the calla lily or Scotch broom business.

Speaking of matters agricultural, the Mendocino area is, unfortunately, best known in many places for its number one cash crop, which happens to be, well, quasi-legal at best. A few years ago, the county's chief agricultural officer listed the estimated value of the marijuana harvest in his annual report, maintaining that it would be unrealistic to ignore it, because it not only was there, it was quite possibly the leading factor in the agricultural economy of the area. The poor man suffered much criticism and never officially mentioned the name of the vile weed again. But it didn't go away. Indeed, it is widely acknowledged to be, at $35 billion, California's largest cash crop, bigger than fruit, vegetables, and wine grapes combined. In 2010, California defeated a measure that would have legalized marijuana. While it was widely believed that legalization would result in a lower price, and be harmful to the Mendocino economy, Mendocino County defeated the measure by 6%, and it lost by 7% statewide. While there were many "Yes" or "No" election signs posted in Mendocino City, there was no graffiti at all (although there was plenty in Fort Bragg). Could it be that even the 'taggers' respect the beauty of Mendocino?

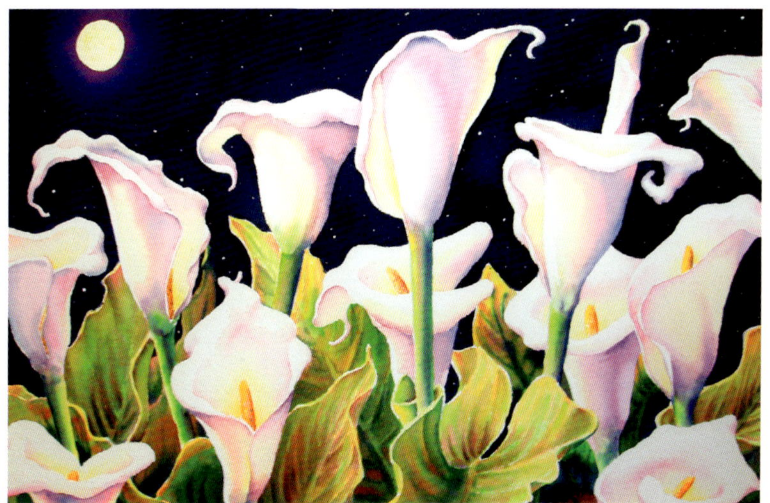

Moonlit Lilies, watercolor

Speaking of cell phones (well now we are), in Mendocino, they are more controversial than in most places, both for their disruptive presence and whatever nasty radiation they may dispense. In 2004, following heated debate, the county supervisors voted 3-2 to keep cell phone towers out of the Mendocino area. By 2011, there was, at best, very limited and erratic service from out-of-town towers, although for those who can't do without, some hotels offer cell phone service through an Internet connection.

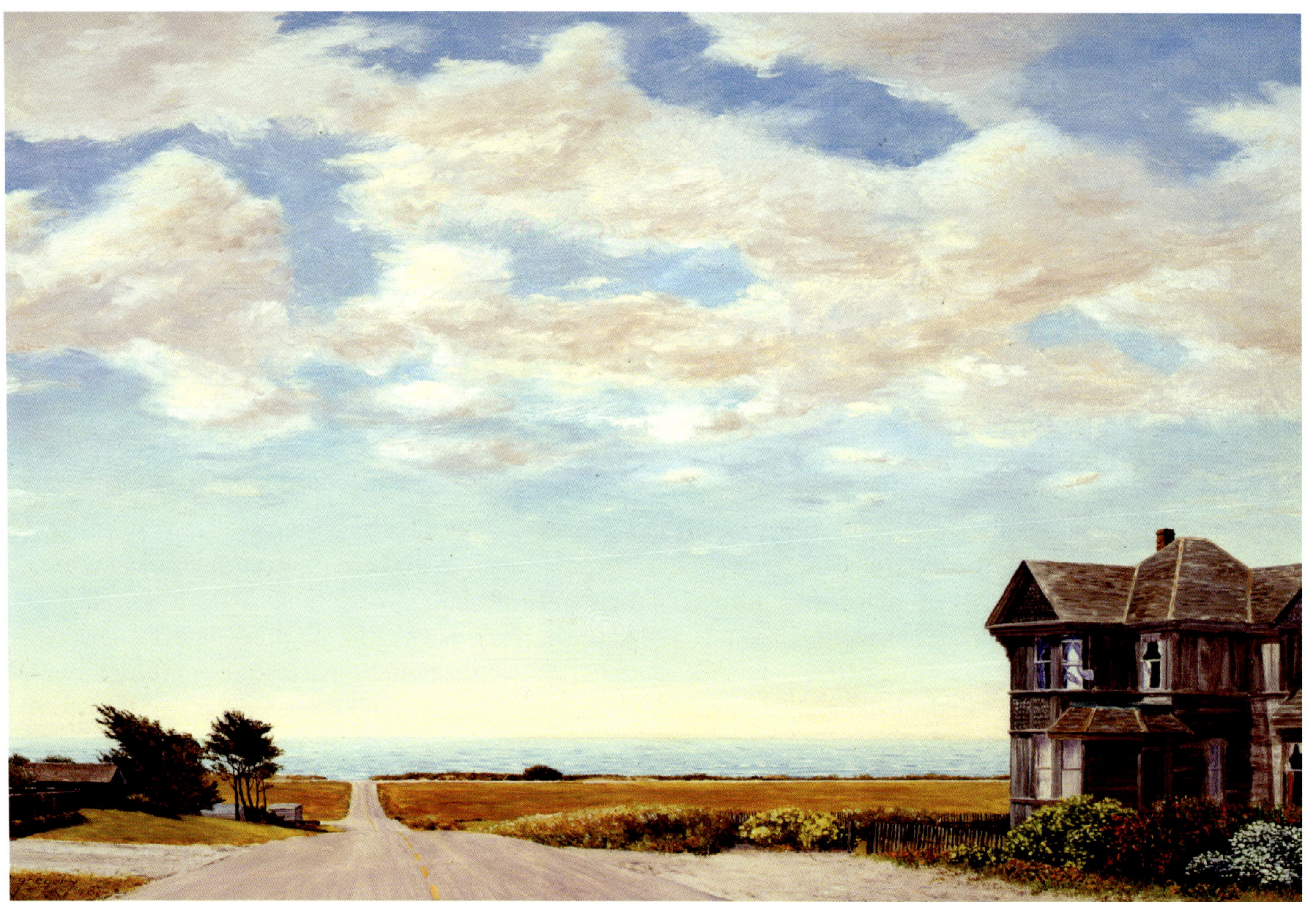

Windy Day, oil

This fine old house, the last one on Little Lake Street, is a reminder that not everyone loves Mendocino. Our neighbors, when we lived in England, were a middle-aged couple whose dream in life was to move from their remote rural village to America, so their twelve year old daughter could have a good education and a bright future. We figured out how to get them to Mendocino, where they could work in our candy store and little factory.

They took the first airplane flight of their lives, and came to Mendocino. It became clear at once that everything was wrong. The cars were too big. The gardens were too small. The people were too informal (they flinched when a clerk at Mendosas addressed them by their first names). Worst of all was this house, which for them was symbolic of everything wrong with Mendocino and America. "How could the owner let it get into this condition," they wailed. "Is there no pride of ownership?" We explained that many people *like* the look of weathered redwood. This was not the *Leave It to Beaver* America of their dreams. They lasted six weeks and headed home. Three years later, their daughter ran off with a Pakistani tee shirt merchant.

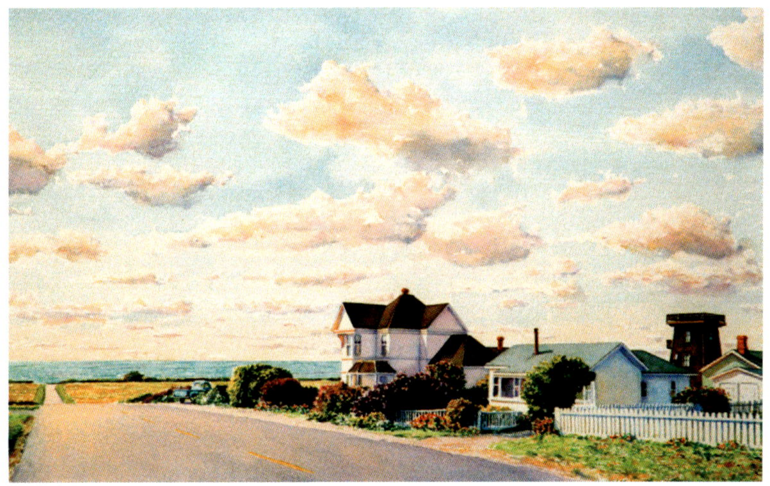

Headlands Houses, watercolor

Here's the trivia quiz you've been waiting for. If these two paintings had been done ten years earlier, what large ugly objects would have been included? No, you don't have to go to page 99; I'll tell you. Telephone poles. After more than a century of wishing and asking, especially by people whose views were filtered through thick black cables, everything was buried underground. And since nothing happens here without some controversy, there were people who objected on the grounds of "Where will the birds sit?" Uh, trees, perhaps?

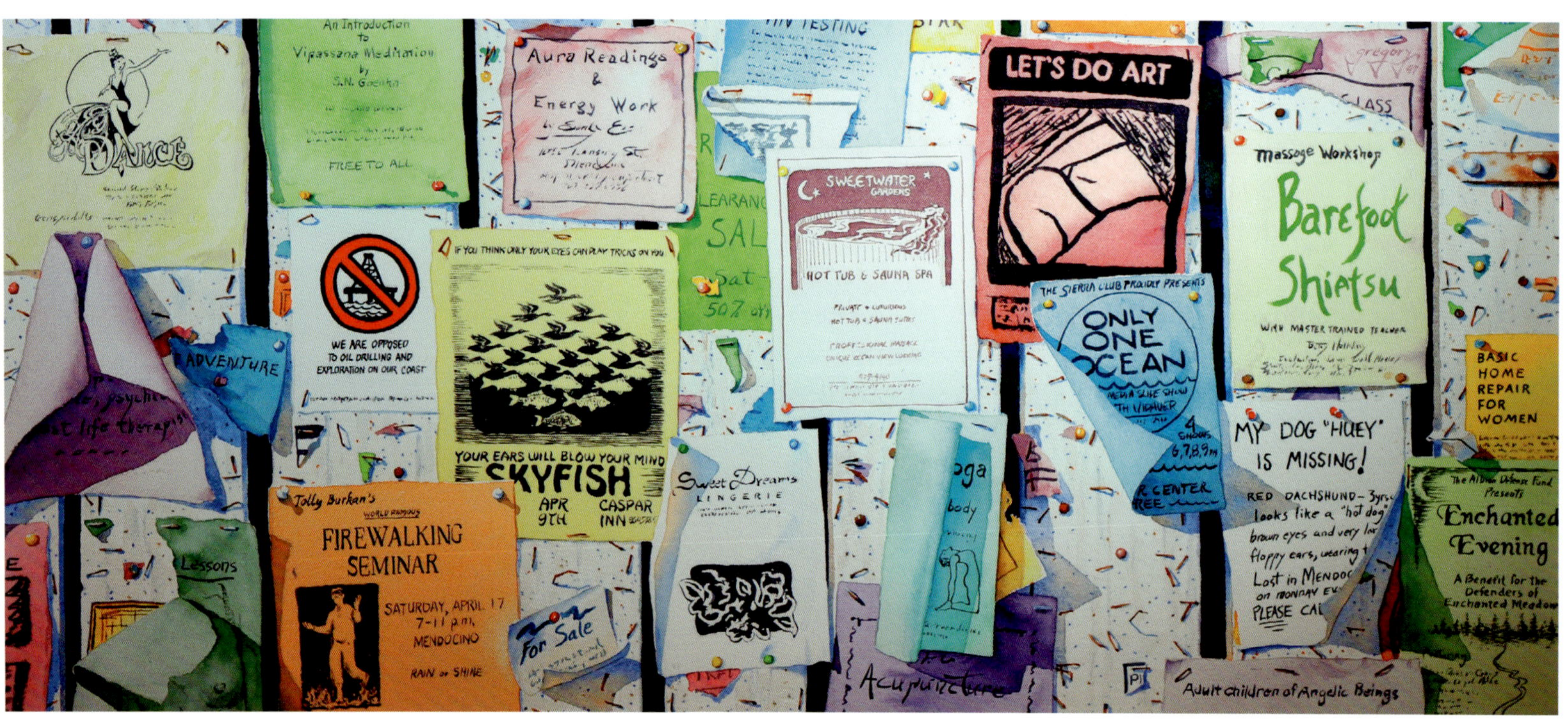

Let's Do Art, watercolor

If all you did was read the bulletin boards and the signs in windows, you'd think you were in a fair-sized city. There's just an awful lot going on in this remote and sparsely-populated place. On a recent weekend, Matthew Fox was speaking in town and Eric Burdon and the Animals were playing at the nearby Navarro Store, and that's just for starters. Bonnie Raitt, John Lee Hooker, Gene Parsons, Flappoid Smatherfoot, and Johnny Winter are among the many 'names' that have performed locally.

More than a few celebrities have lived in (or allegedly lived in) or certainly dined in the vicinity, from Truman Capote to Booker T (apparently without the MGs). Madonna and Sean Penn honeymooned here, and while it was hard not to notice them, people gave them their privacy, as they have done with many others. A near exception was the time Robert Redford was standing at the back of the Cafe Beaujolais discussing the next day's menu with the proprietor. One diner could barely restrain himself. Summoning his waiter, he gushed, "Is that ... is that who I think it is?" The waiter, without missing a beat, replied, "Yes, that's Margaret Fox, but I don't know who that is with her."

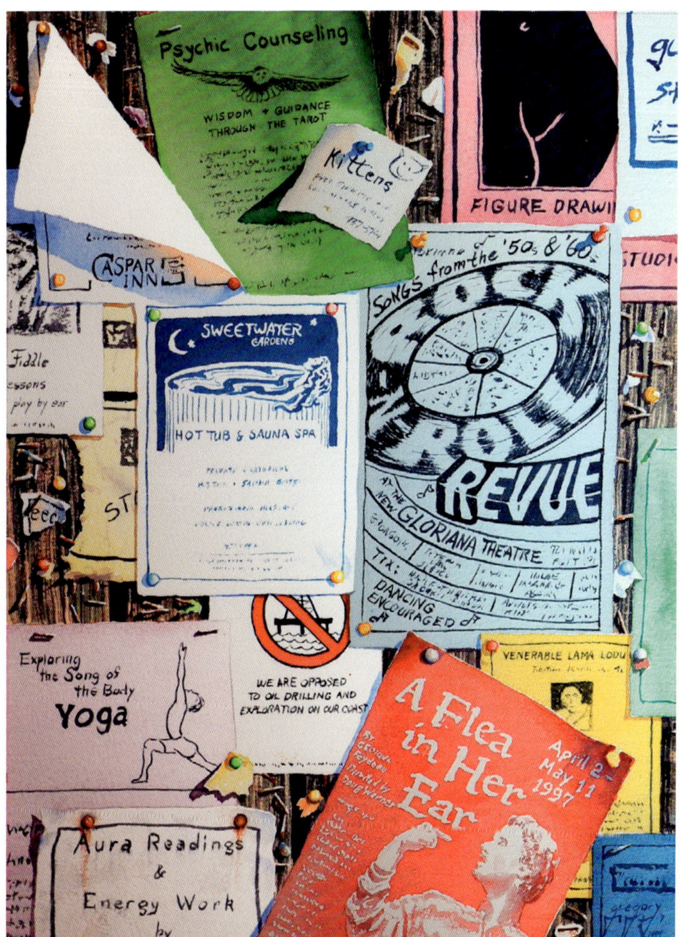

A Flea in Her Ear, watercolor

The name of the Lisbon House evokes the memory of the many Portuguese people who contributed to the growth and development of Mendocino, both in the early days and through to the present. An advertisement in 1887 read, "Go to the Lisbon House and get a square meal for 25 cents. The best table in town. Beds 25 cents. Antone Fernandez, Proprietor."

Many settlers–Fernandez, Mendosa, Gomez, Fayal, Silva, Lemos, and others–came to the United States on whaling ships from Portugal and from the Azores islands off the Portuguese coast. Some settled first on the east coast or in Hawaii but eventually came to Mendocino where land was cheap and jobs were plentiful.

Curiously, no streets in Mendocino have Portuguese names, but the area where many of the homes were built has long been known as Portuguese (or "Portugee") flats.

The Lisbon House deck has an especially pleasant vista, and is in itself a worthy example of the decorative woodcrafters art.

Mendocino has a long history of skilled woodworking, beginning with the mill workers of the 1870s whose artistic sense compelled them to do more than just make long straight boards. Happily for builders today, the same turning, carving and scrollwork skills are readily available, building on the legacy of James Krenov.

Krenov was a Siberian-born, China-raised, Swedish-trained master woodworker and furniture builder. In the 1970s, he came to Mendocino, first to teach, then to settle down and establish a fine woodworking program at the College of the Redwoods. Students and crafts people came from all over to learn from the master. He died in 2009 holding a piece of wood in his hand, and was buried at sea. The unusual and superbly built furniture and decorative wood items displayed at several local galleries are a part of his legacy.

The area's other master woodworker was Dean Stephens, a builder of wooden boats, who moved to the coast in 1971, settling on the Abalobadiah Ranch. He established a rigorous program, in which 22 students lived on the ranch for two years working 14-hour days, each building a wooden sailboat.

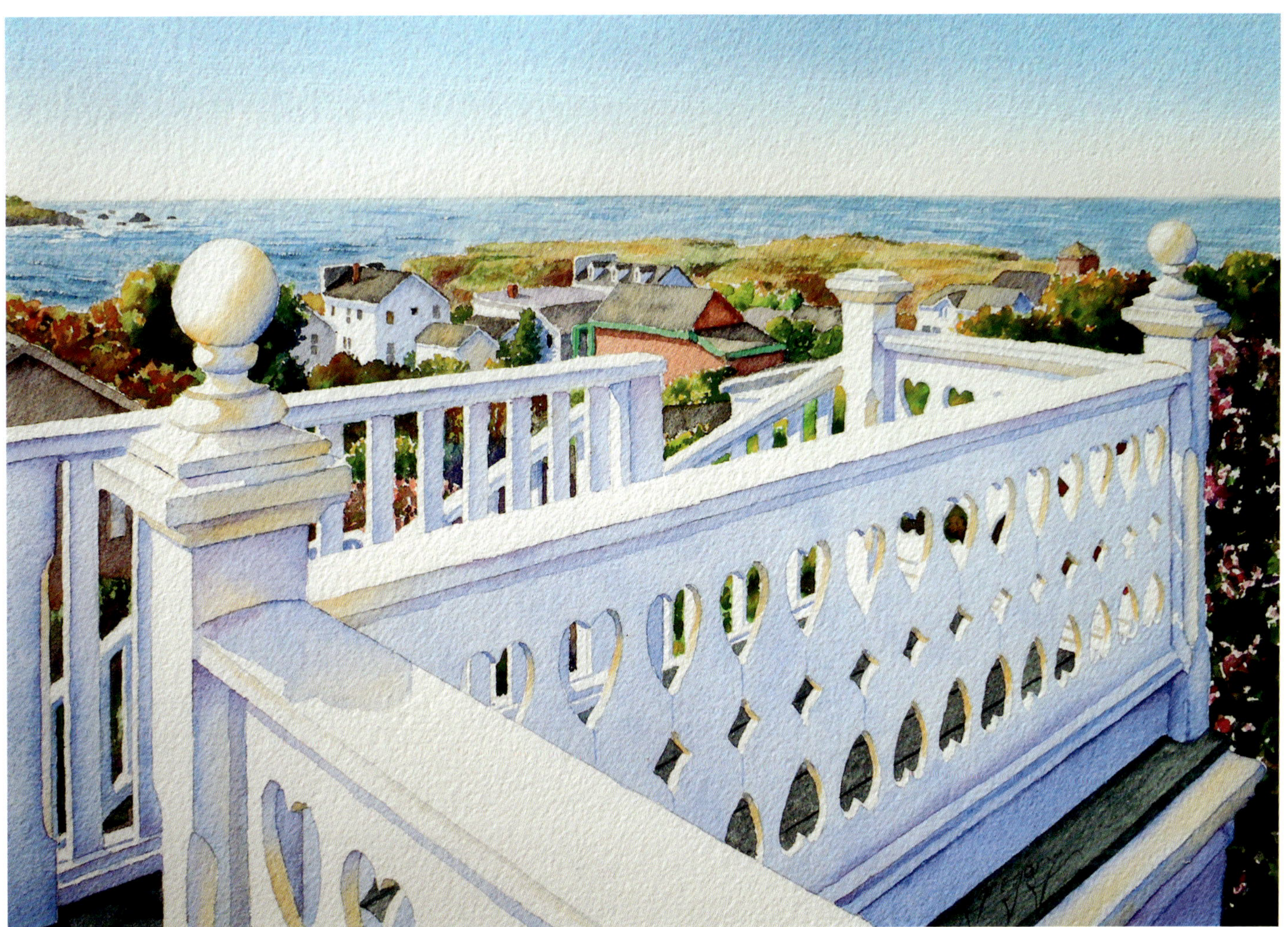

View From Lisbon House, watercolor

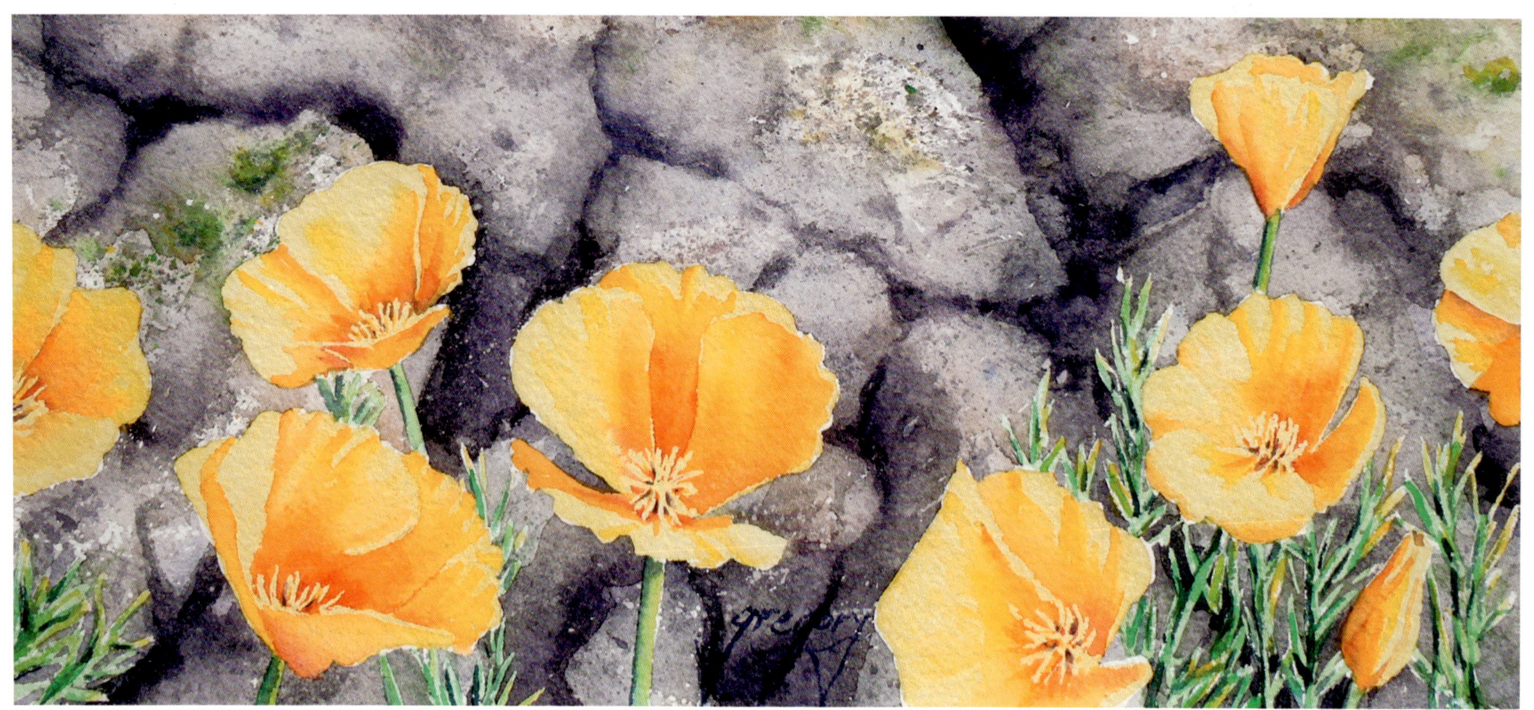

California Poppies, watercolor

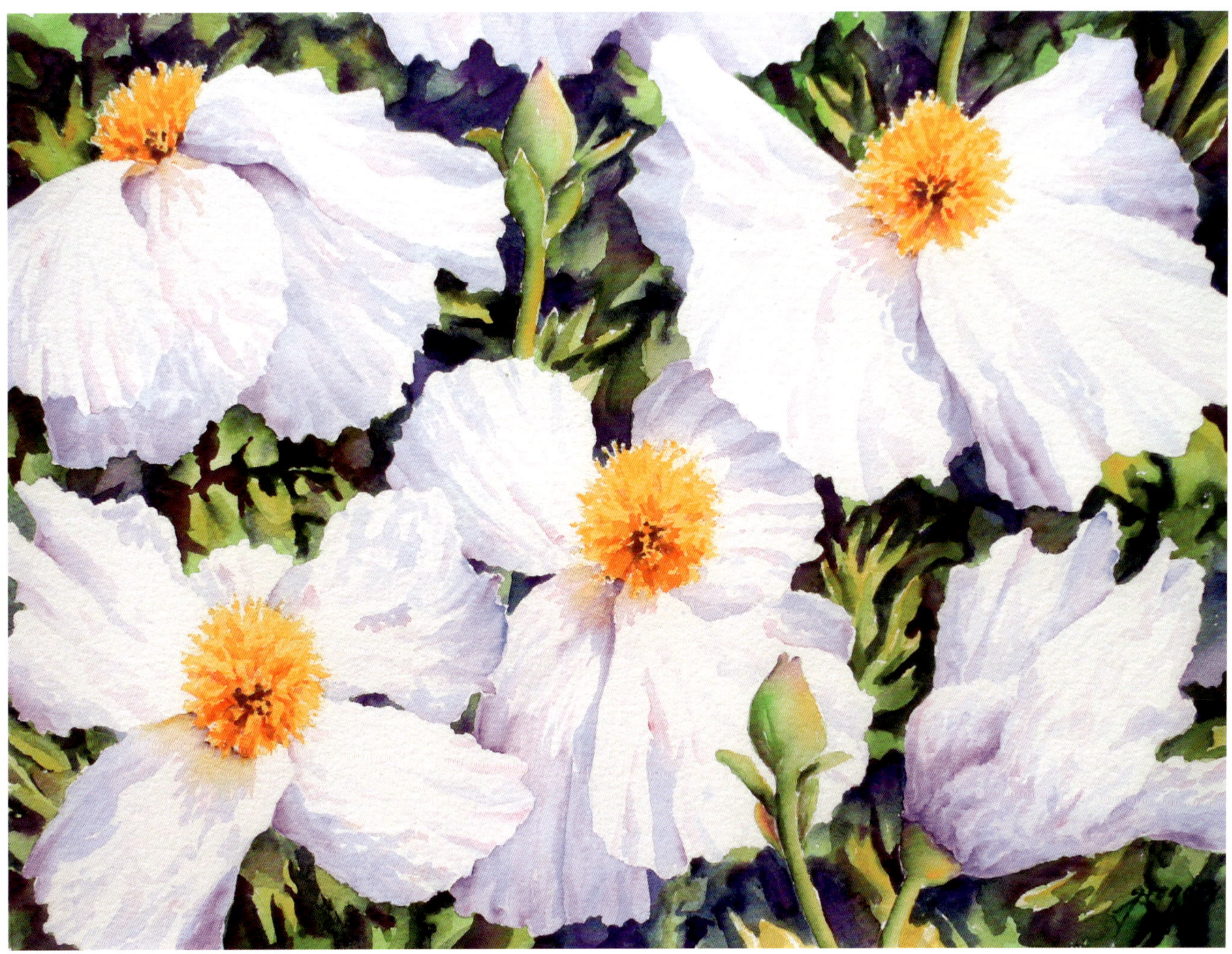

Matilja Poppies, watercolor

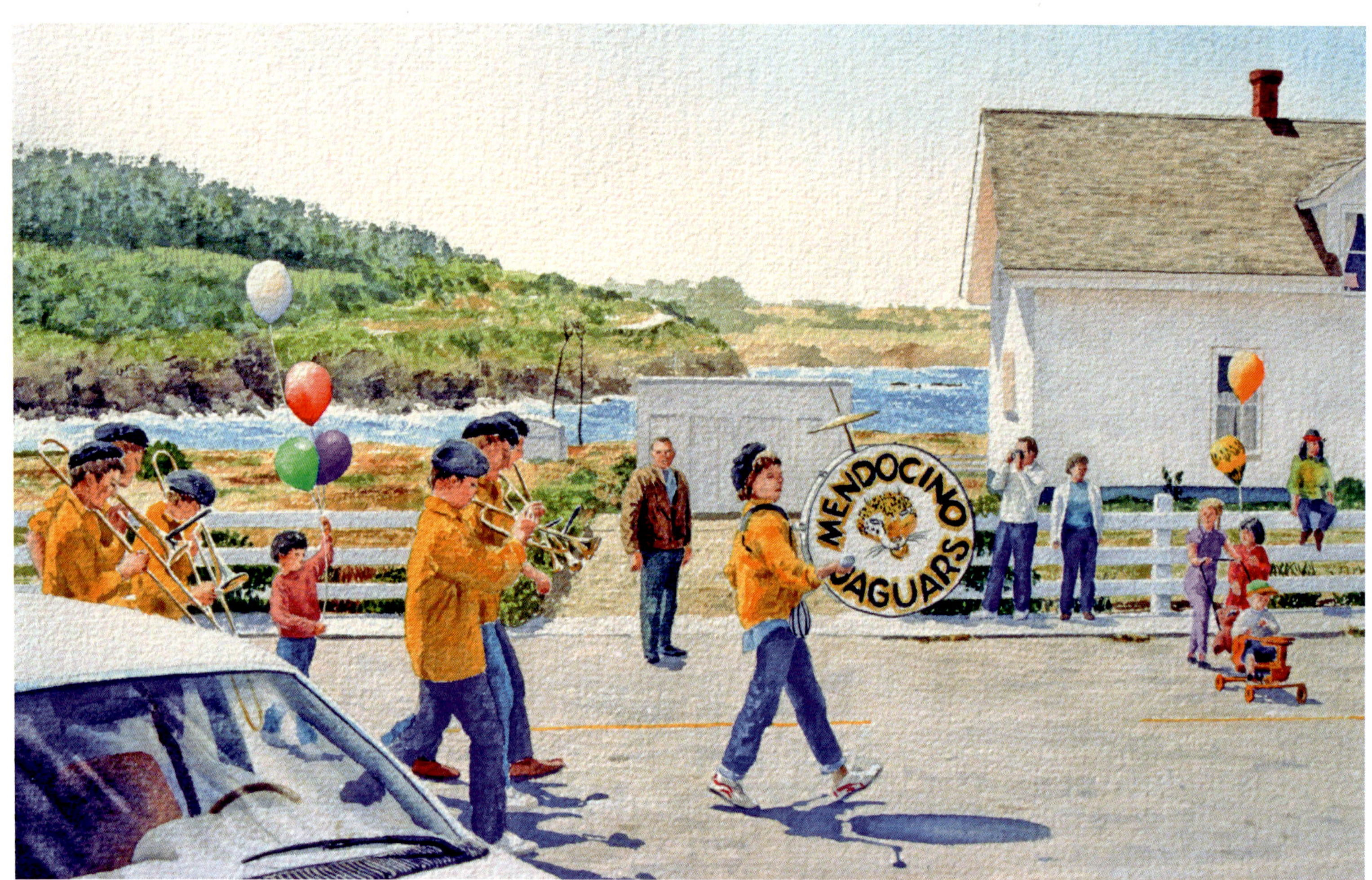

Parade, watercolor

Mendocino is blessed with an unusually good school system. The middle school was chosen by the U.S. Department of Education as one of the outstanding public schools in the country, but it, along with its marching band and mascot, is no more. The 7th and 8th grades were incorporated into a new K-8 school, and the 9th grade joined the high school. Old timers will recognize the gentleman standing to the left of the drummer, the late *Beacon* columnist Jack Helfer.

When our family, with three little girls, was ready to move from England back to America in the mid 1970's, we wrote to dozens of school districts around the country, asking questions about their facilities, philosophy of education, and enrichment programs. Not only did the one detailed and substantial reply come from Mendocino, but principals from other districts wrote to say, in effect, "Don't come here; go to Mendocino. That's what I would do." And so we did and never regretted it. The scenery and tranquility were added bonuses.

Community interest in the schools is erratic. It has always been hard to get people to turn out for PTA or athletic boosters club meetings. But when a group of conservative citizens petitioned the school board for the removal of the grammar school principal (who wore both a beard and a peace symbol), hundreds of people turned out to voice their support of one side or the other. Because the anti-principal people called themselves the Concerned Parents League, the principal and I renamed our small but active bowling group The Concerned Bowlers League, and we have the embroidered shirts to prove it. (The principal was retained, but a few years later, he moved to a non-administrative position.)

One thing we found especially interesting about the schools is that they are probably as close to a classless society as anything Karl Marx envisioned. When our children were invited to the home of friends, there was no way they (or we) could predict in advance whether we would find them living in an oceanfront mansion, a rusty converted school bus in the woods, or anything in between. The school district is sparsely populated but is very large, stretching nearly 50 miles over the hills to the east. Some children spend as much as three hours a day on the school bus.

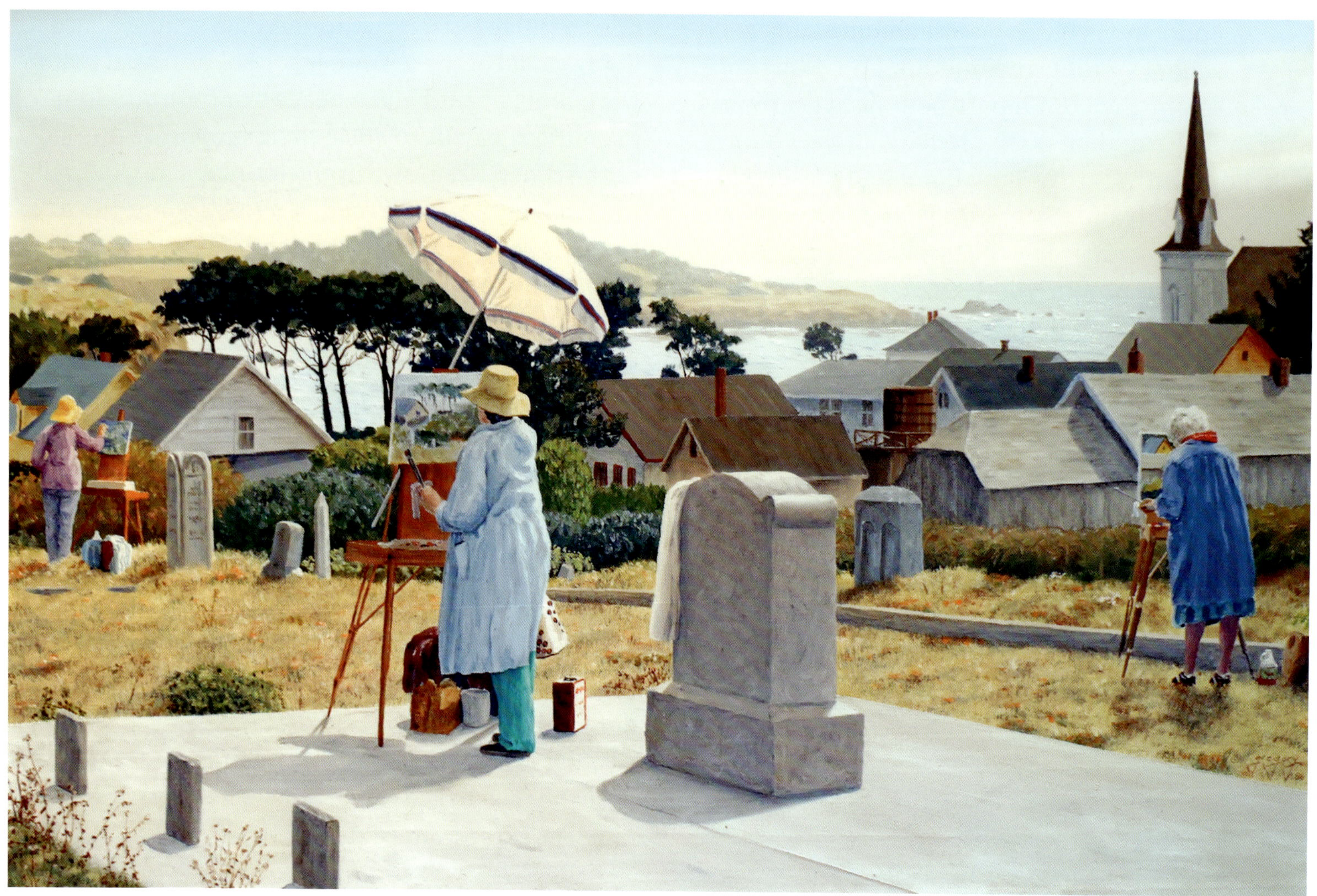

Painting the Town, oil

Mendocino is supremely paintable. People of all ages and skill levels can be found at work almost any day of the year. While artists first discovered Mendocino in the 19th century, interest in the arts began flourishing with the establishment of the Mendocino Art Center by William Zacha and his colleagues in the 1960s. The Art Center has grown into a sizable institution, with an internationally renowned weaving apprenticeship program plus year-round, summer, and weekend courses in painting, pottery, textiles, photography, and other forms of art including computer art.

Over the years, no issue seems to have aroused the populace and caused people to choose up sides as much as the matter of street artists: the painters, sculptors, craftspeople, and musicians who displayed their wares or their talents on the public sidewalks. Some merchants objected to the competition, the noise, or perhaps the very existence of these people.

After heated debate, the Board of Supervisors passed a hastily drawn ordinance forbidding the doing of anything on a public sidewalk in expectation of being paid. Distribution of free literature was permitted.

The first salvo in the battle came with the creation of a poster that at first glance looked like an ordinary travel poster, but read, "Come to Mendocino, the Art Colony that Banned Street Artists." It went on to say, "Come to Mendocino, where you can buy works of art lovingly purchased by local boutique owners at the San Francisco Gift Show."

The second salvo came when a local troublemaker (well, actually it was the author of this very book) set up a vending table outside a gift shop on Main Street, giving away free copies of *Hustler* magazine and selling copies of the Bill of Rights for a nickel. Under the new law, the first was legal, and the second was a criminal offense. The sheriff was informed of this scofflaw activity, and in short order, a deputy arrived to make an arrest.

Judge Lamb, an enlightened local jurist, declared the law unconstitutional. It was rewritten to permit sidewalk vending of printed matter only. And the street artists never returned to the streets of Mendocino.

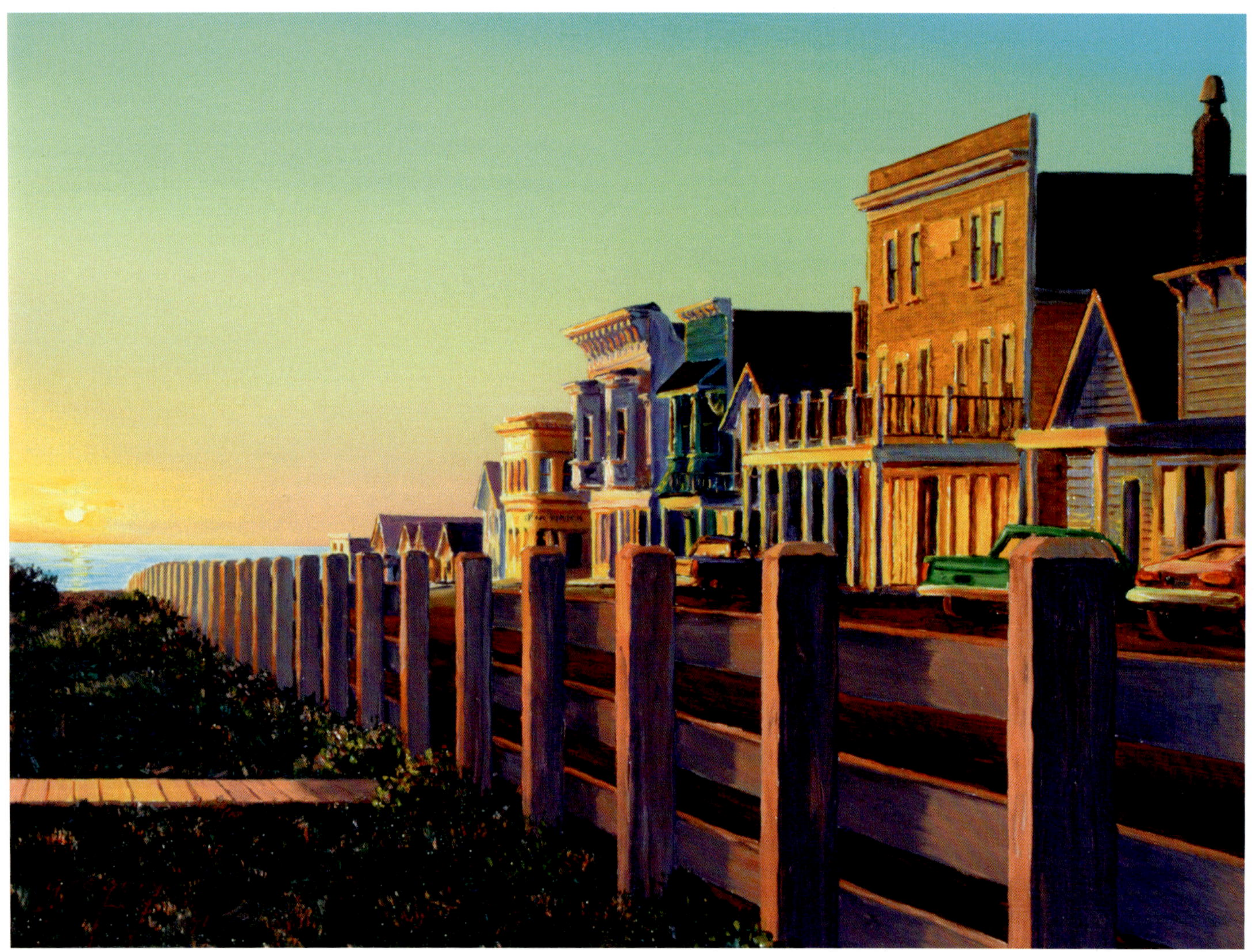

Main Street Sunset, oil

You will not see any more neon signs in Mendocino. The Historical Review Board took care of that. This painting could be said to commemorate the last one, a "Martini" sign outside Dick's Place, an old time Main Street bar.

Sidewalk signs are disallowed as well, but sometimes people try to pass them off as art. A little further west on Main Street was the ice cream parlor opened by some friends[1] and me. We were denied a sign that stuck out from the building, thereby making us hard to find.

So we made a life sized wooden carving of a man enjoying an ice cream cone and placed it on the sidewalk. When we were told to take it down, we declared that it was sidewalk art, which *was* legal. "Then where's the price tag?" they asked. We put one on, and a few days later, sold our "sign" for $300.

(At this writing, that retail space is vacant once again. Something to think about, hmmm?)

1 Two obstetricians, an optometrist, a judge, and two retired Navy Captains: a true Mendocino project.

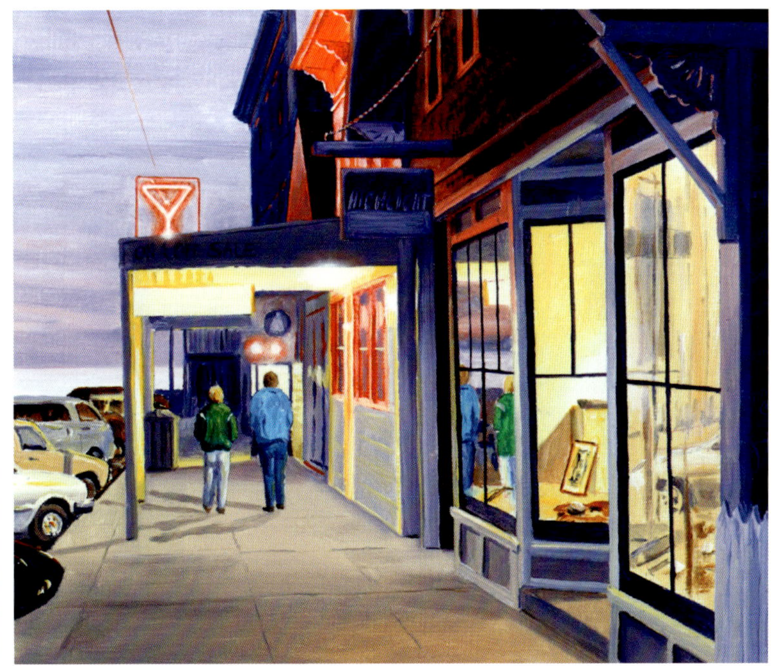

Night Lights (detail), oil

Our ice cream was called Captain Hendershot's Ice Cream, named for the retired Navy captain who ran our little factory. When we sold the business, the new owner (a college professor living his dream of moving to the country) immediately changed the name to The Mendocino Ice Cream Company. It's what people do to capture the magic of the name: Mendocino Pasta, Mendocino Mustard, Mendocino Sea Salt, etc.

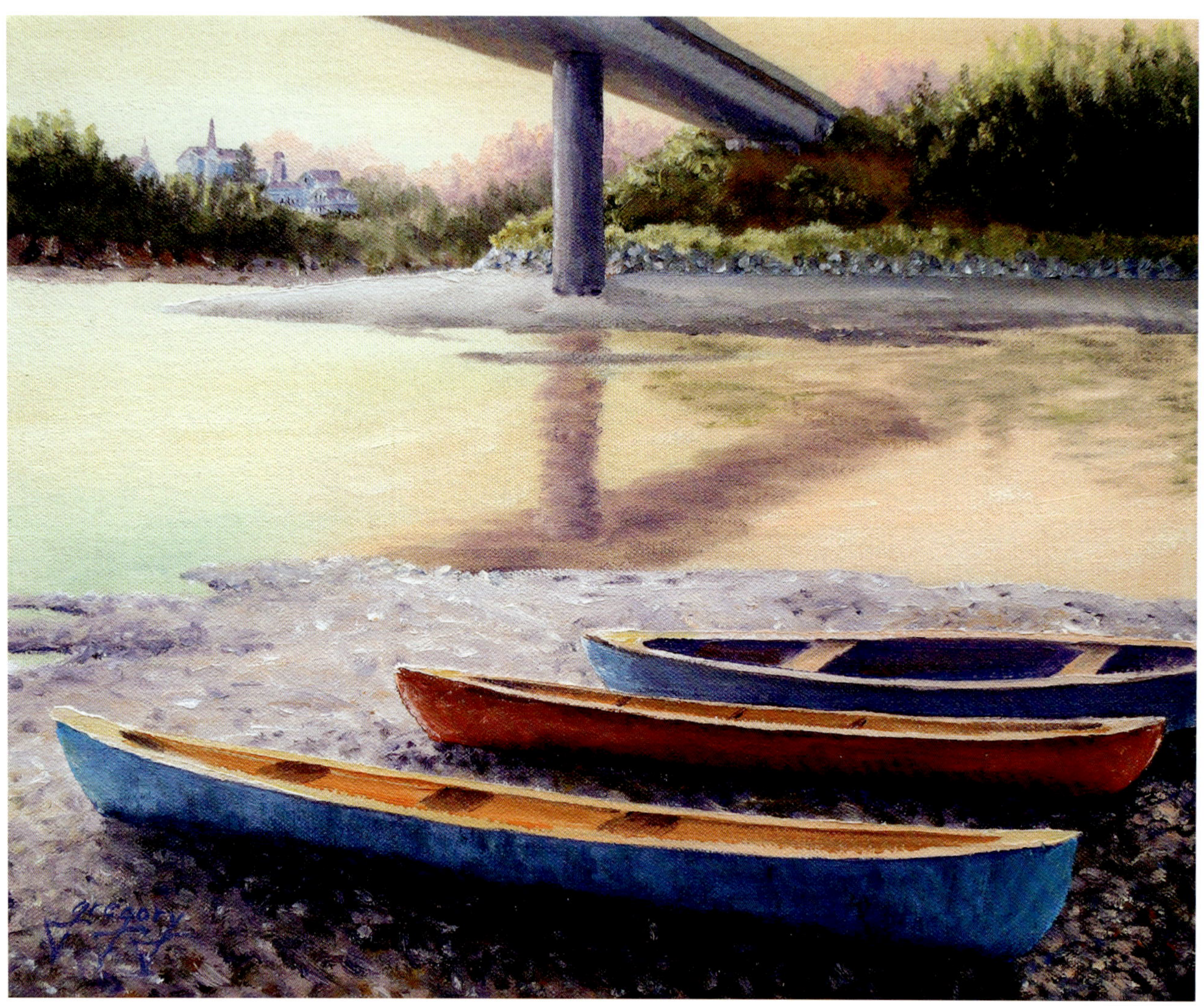

Catch a Canoe, oil

Many a tourist has arrived beguiled by photos of Mendocino's wide sandy beaches, with bikini, sunglasses, and a tanning lotion in hand, only to be forcefully reminded that this is northern California where waterfront action is limited to hiking, kite flying, whale watching, exploring tide pools, picnics around the bonfire, and the like. The first eight miles of Big River is a tidal estuary, which means that if you time it right, you can kayak, canoe or row upstream with the tide, have a nice swim (because it is warmer there) and a picnic, and let the tide assist you on the trip back to Big River beach.

The 7,000 acres adjoining the river was purchased from the timber company in 2002: a marvel of cooperation among federal and state agencies, nonprofit corporations, and thousands of individual donors.

Catch A Canoe, originally the Mendocino Yacht and Canoe Club, specializes in redwood outrigger canoes, handmade in Mendocino's Secret Harbor Boat Works. Dogs are welcome to ride in the canoes, and, indeed, to dine at the elegant and extremely dog-friendly adjoining resort, Stanford Inn by the Sea. While the law prevents dogs in restaurants, they are permitted in hotel lobbies — and the Stanford Inn has cleverly built a very large lobby, and outfitted it with chairs and tables, so that it closely resembles a dining room. It is charming to see many folks enjoying their splendid vegan breakfasts, with their faithful dogs at their feet gnawing on a veggie-bone.

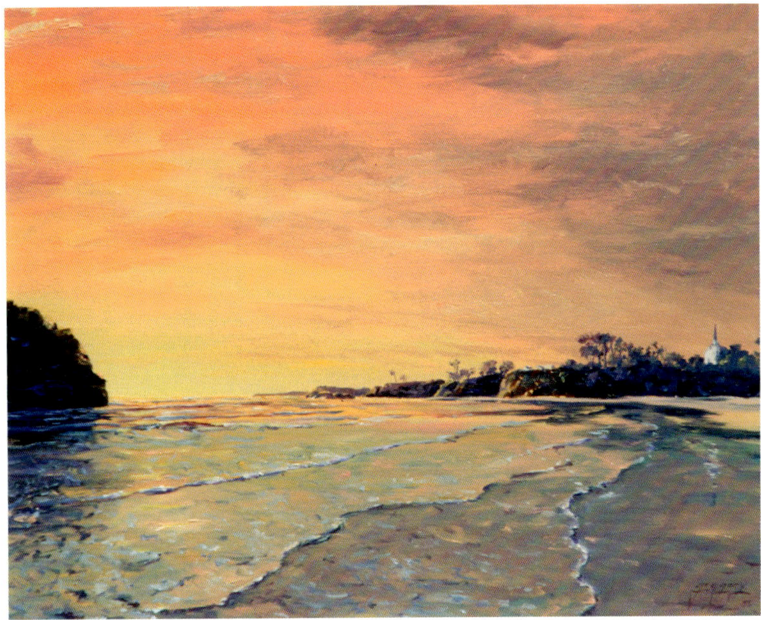

Big River Sunset, oil

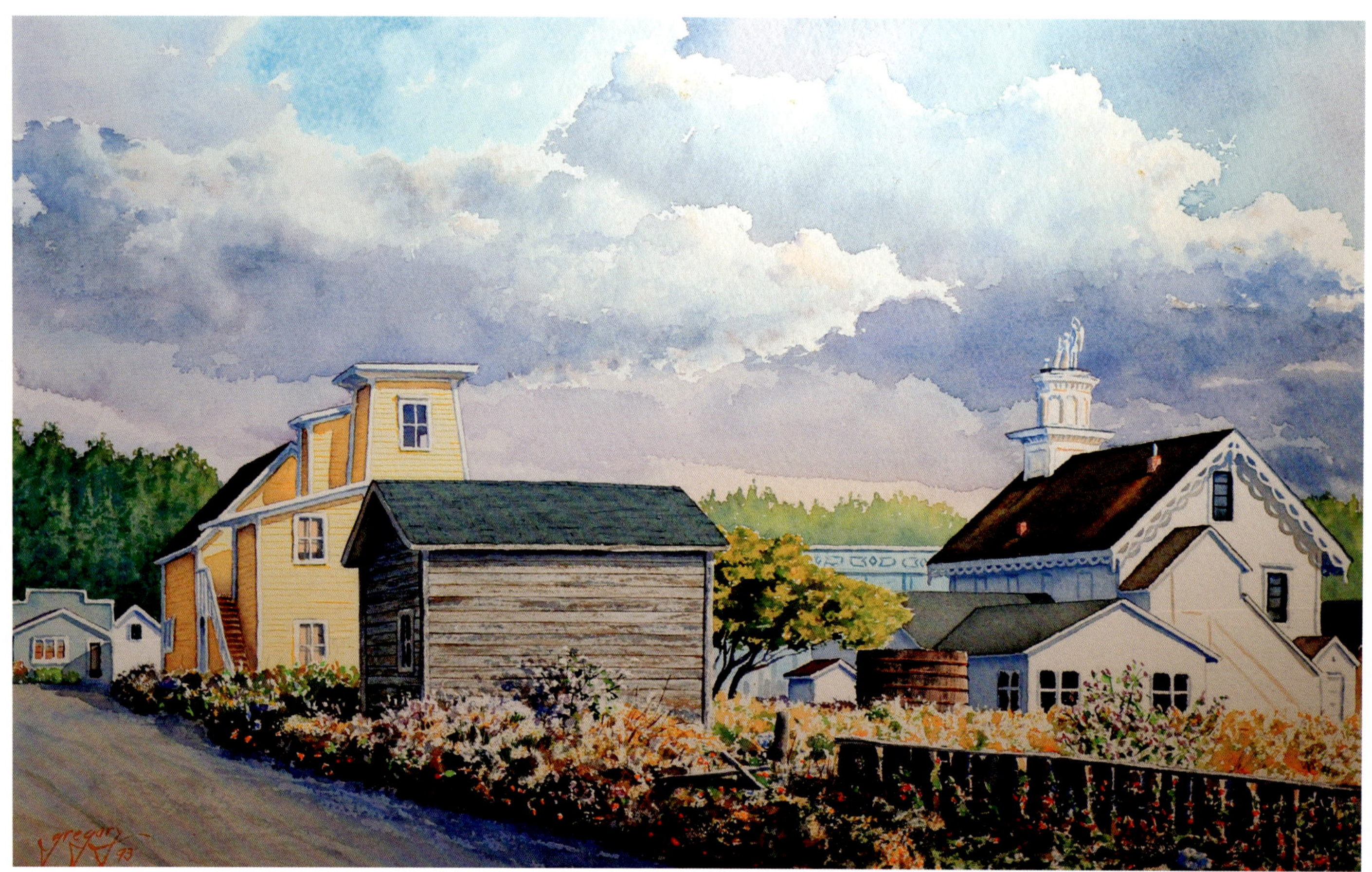

Storm Clouds, watercolor

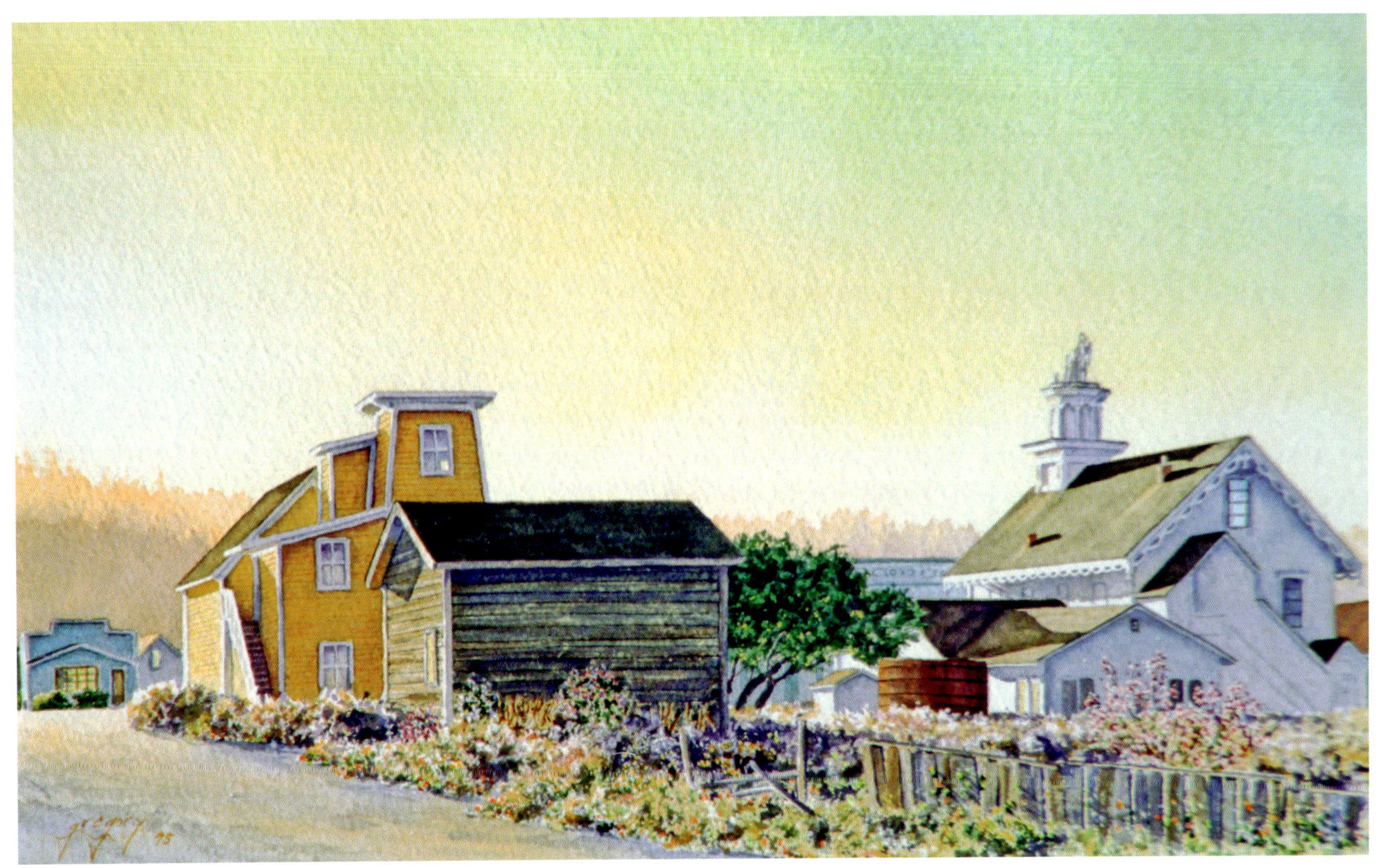

A Clear Day, watercolor

Following the 1906 San Francisco earthquake, huge amounts of redwood were shipped from the mills along the Mendocino coast, and that meant increased ship traffic and a need for a lighthouse (or light station, as they were called then) at the dangerous Point Cabrillo, just north of town. The best part of this Light Station is the amazing fresnel lens, endlessly pulsing and turning. Unless you are well connected, you cannot go into the tower to see it operating[1] (but there is live television camera pointed at it, so you can watch the monitor in the gift shop). The California Coastal Conservancy, which saved this area from developers in 1992, has restored two original lighthouse keepers' homes, and rents them to the public.

Disquieting news: as we go to press in 2011, the state says Pt. Cabrillo will close *permanently* in 2012 to save a few dollars. For the record, the cost of fighting the war in Afghanistan for 23 seconds would keep Pt. Cabrillo open for a year.

"Saved from the developers." That's a phrase we say a fair amount, and some wish we could say more. As Abraham Maslow famously said, "If you're a hammer, everything looks like a nail." And if you're a developer, every piece of oceanfront land looks like a hotel, a restaurant, a housing development, or a casino. Also in 1992 a plan to cut down many trees, dam a stream, and build a convention center on 36 acres in Mendocino was rejected (vote of 4 to 1) by the Board of Supervisors.

1 Hey, we put you in our book. Now can we see it?

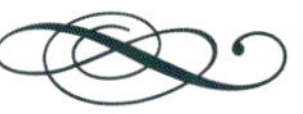

Abalone used to be plentiful off the Mendocino coast. But with abalone meat now selling for four times the price of a good steak, and the iridescent shells more in demand for jewelry and crafts, poaching has become a major problem. You can collect up to three abalone a day, a maximum of 24 per year, and they must be at least 7 inches across. Even though rangers with powerful binoculars patrol the cliffs and the headlands, and a local Abalone Watch group stands guard, and even though the penalties can be severe, more and more people (most of them, it seems, from the Bay Area) are willing to take the chance. Each week's *Beacon* has a lengthy "Court Reporter" section, in which the names and specific offenses of the perpetrators are all listed, along with their fines, typically in the four digits.

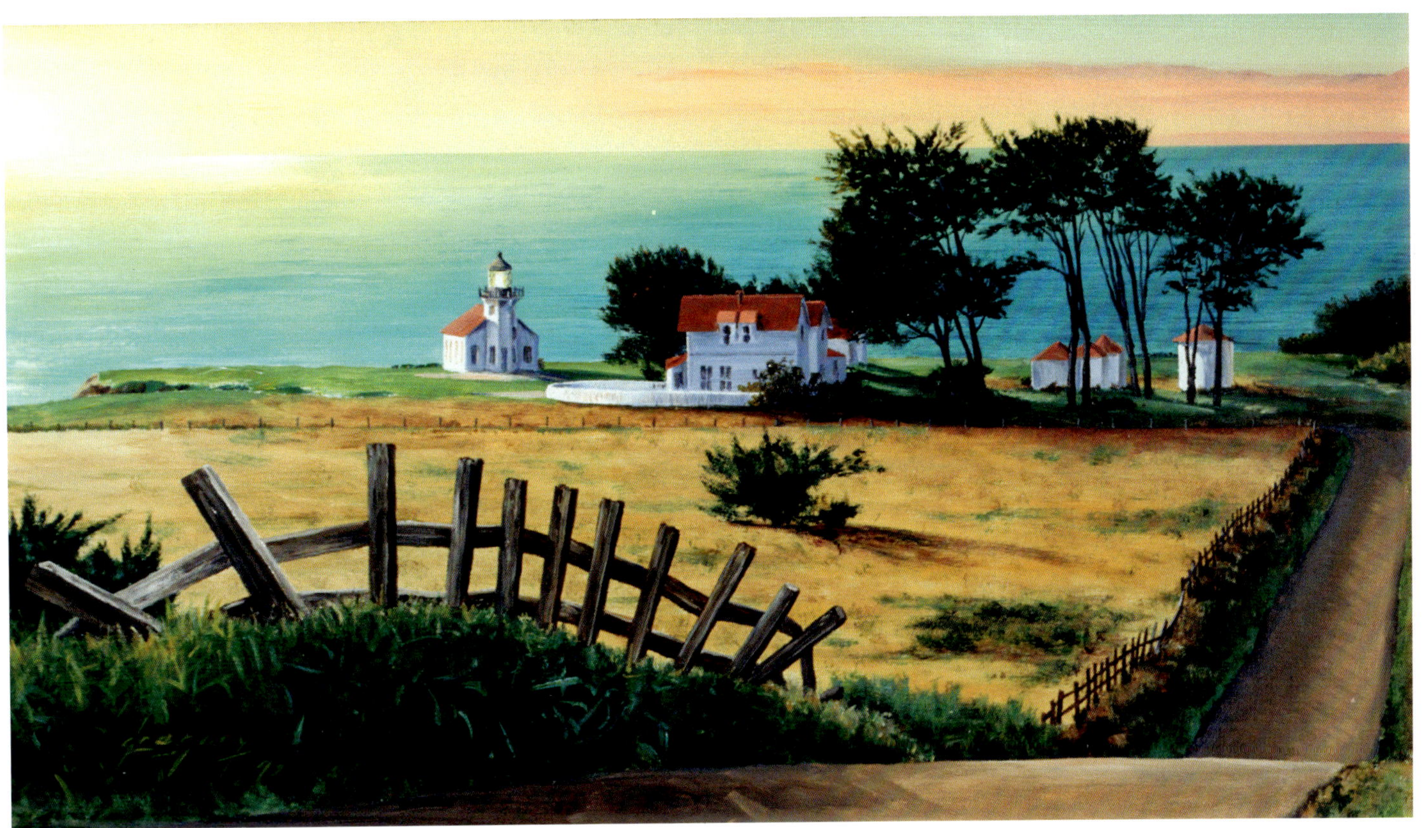

Point Cabrillo Lighthouse, oil

Noyo is the home of Thanksgiving Coffee, one of the few coffee roasting factories in Northern California, and pioneer buyer of politically correct (fair trade, shade-grown, organic) coffee. When the wind is right, splendid odors even reach the cars crossing the main highway bridge over Noyo harbor—a distinct improvement over the fish processing factory. Other unique aspects of the Noyo harbor area include a restaurant featuring shrimp wonton, and another offering 24-ounce hamburgers. Noyo is also the home of the Noyo Food Forest, a network of local farmers, teachers, children, artists, chefs, and others, dedicated to being the change they wish to see in the world, through education, social enterprise, and community involvement. They have turned blighted vacant lots into gardens, producing tons of food for the community.

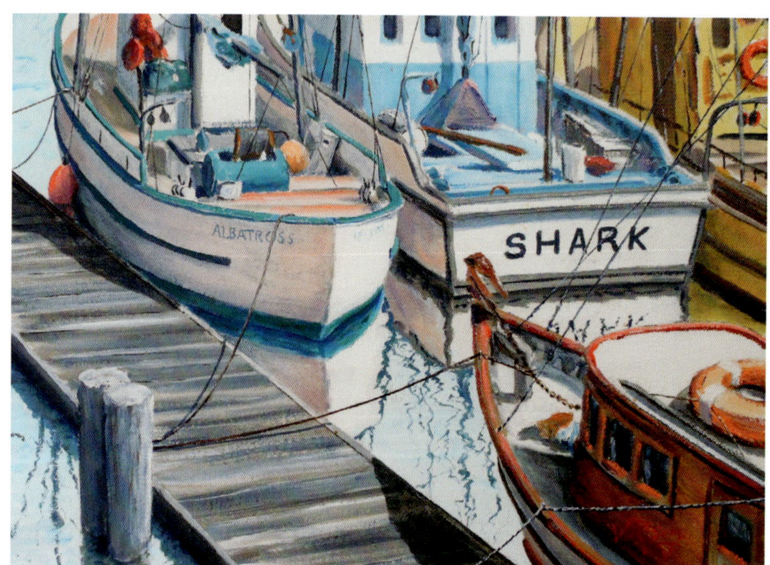

Noyo Boats, oil

Once Roger Corman's film company came to Noyo to make what they declared would be a serious science-fiction horror film. The plot dealt with an experiment to create a new breed of salmon at the Noyo salmon breeding station. But something goes wrong, resulting in the creation of half-man half-salmon creatures who rise out of the Noyo River to chase after local women with whom they wish to mate. Many local people had roles in this extravaganza, but it turned out to be so dreadful the producers ended up declaring that it really was a spoof after all. It lasted about three days in the movie centers of America, but you can still rent copies of *Humanoids from the Deep* at your local video store, probably because of the scenes of half-man half-salmon monsters chasing half-naked ladies on Noyo beach.

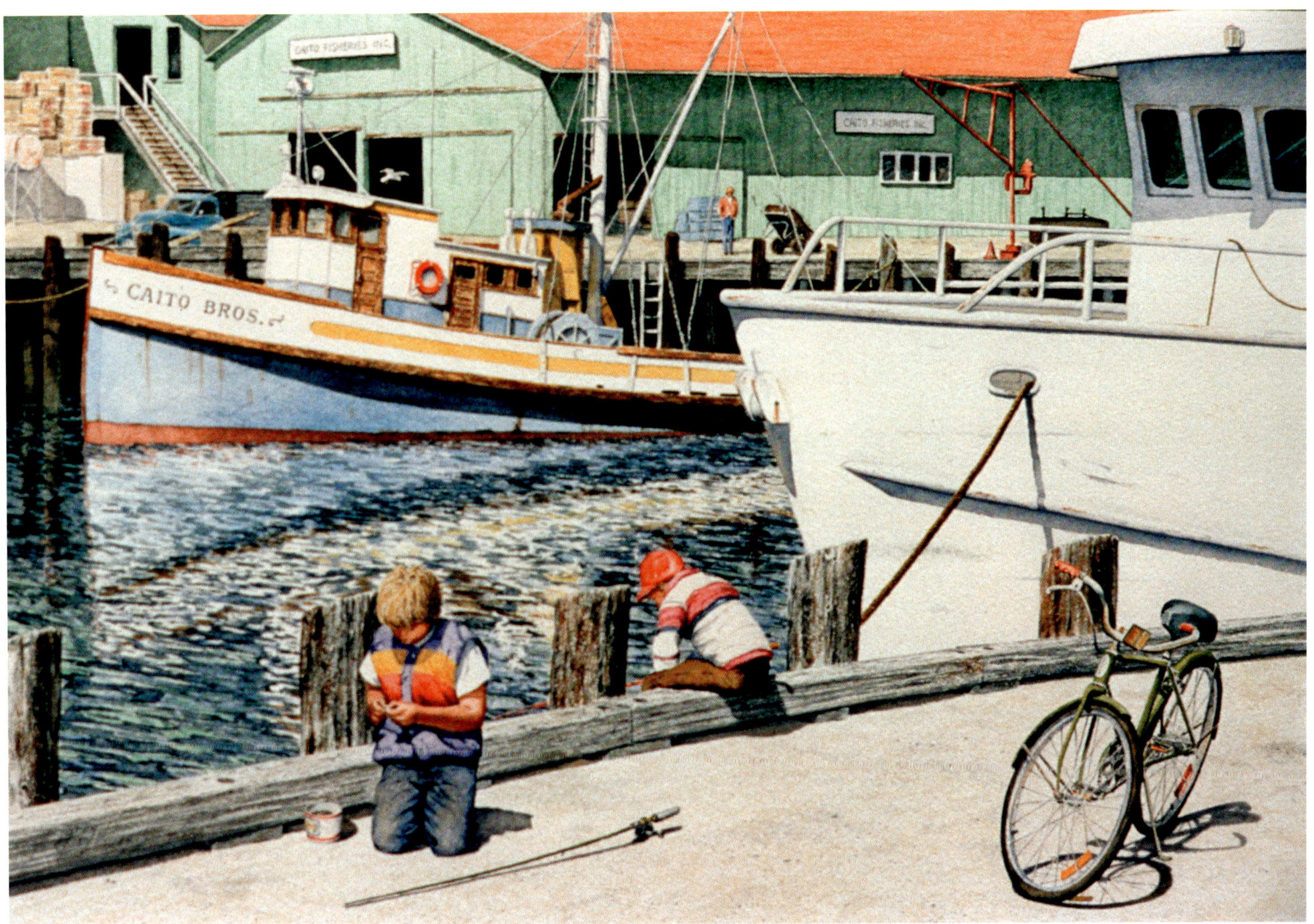

Brothers, watercolor

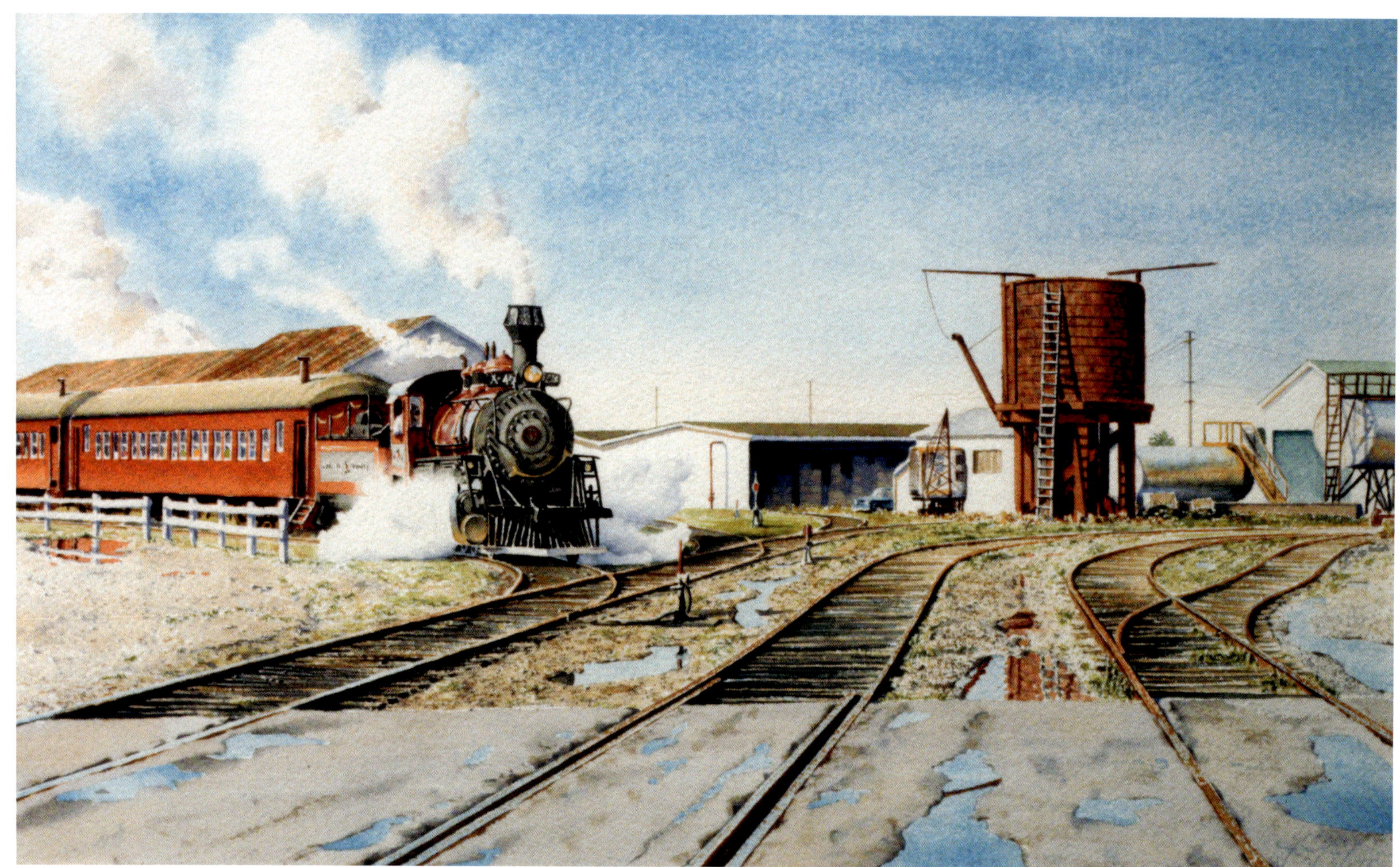

Skunk Train, watercolor

Trains are generally much more fun to watch (and paint) from the outside than to ride on the inside. When you're zipping along the rails at 29 miles an hour, it hardly matters if you're being pulled by diesel, gasoline, or the splendid steam engine. But when you're standing by the track, whether on a Fort Bragg sidewalk or deep in a redwood forest, and the mighty Baldwin engine chugs past, now that's a great train experience.

What was originally the Fort Bragg Railroad, then, charmingly, the California Western Railroad and Navigation Company, and now simply the Skunk Train™ (yes, we all know, 'you smell it before you see it') was established in 1885 to haul logs from the inland forest to the coastal mill. For quite a few years, it looked as if the steam rides were gone forever, but in 2005, old #45 steamed back to life for occasional runs during the busy times of the year.

When Marina and I operated the Flying Bear Candy Store and Factory, just across Main Street from the Skunk depot, we used to reverse the window fan just as the train pulled in each day with its cargo of tourists, thereby blanketing the neighborhood with the odors of freshly-made peanut brittle or English toffee: a powerful aromatic magnet that pulled those people across the street and into the store.

One day, a local man, a regular, pointed to our chocolate-covered Brazil nuts, and said, "Give me a pound of those n****r toes." Hey, they didn't teach us how to handle that in sales clerk class. I was truly offended, but said nothing, and silently filled the order. The next time this guy came in, we were ready. Marina had made a batch of *white*-chocolate-covered Brazil nuts, and when the same request was made, I could say, "We don't make those any more. Would you like some honky toes?"

We got to know our customers by their taste buds, not by their names. Eventually we learned that the "two pounds of dark maples" man was the local pharmacist, and the "one pound, assorted, leave out the caramels" woman was a county supervisor. And when we put the business up for sale, it was nearly bought by a local dentist, who had the idea of running an ethical candy store: a row of sinks by the door, with disposable toothbrushes: you had to brush and floss before you could leave.

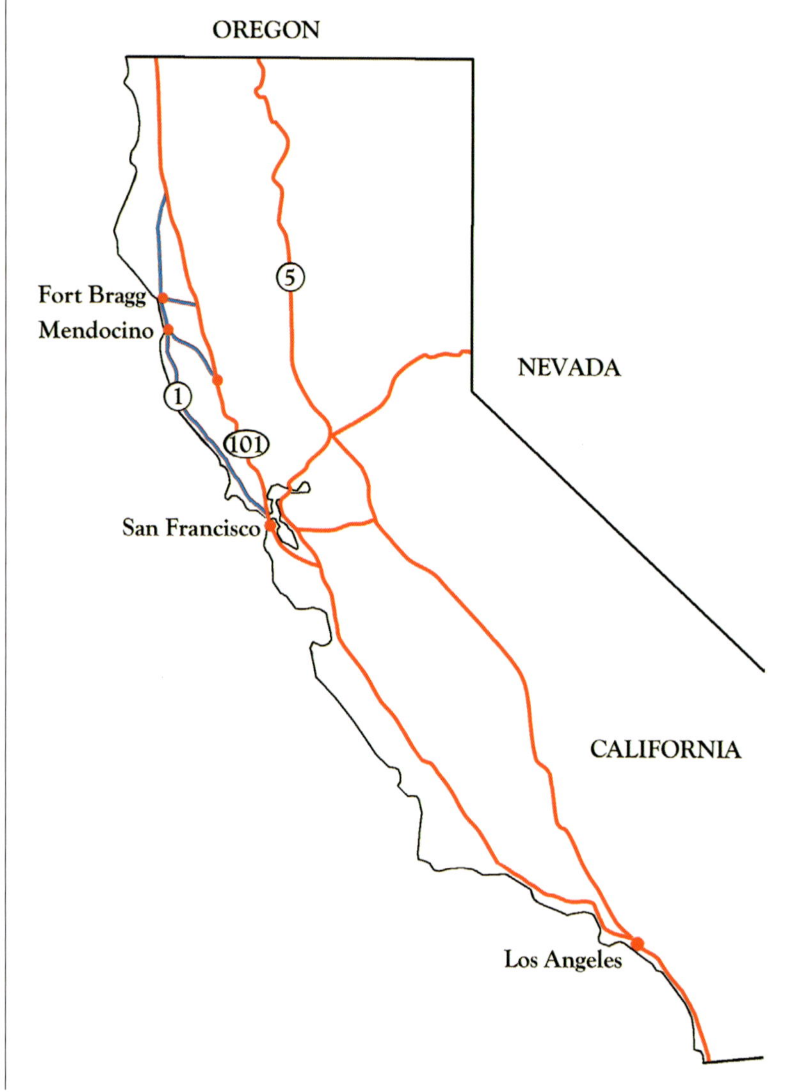

There are only 21 street names in all of Mendocino, so you would think we would know them all. A tourist once asked to be directed to Carlson Street and the four of us, representing over 100 person-years of living in Mendocino, had no idea where it was. But then they identified the person they were seeking, and of course all of us were instantly able to provide detailed directions, and we could have reported (but didn't) that he had a new girlfriend, was having financial problems, and was hitting the sauce. There's not a lot of privacy in Mendocino City.

So that you can locate the sites of some of the paintings you have seen in this book, here is a map on the opposite page (a reminder that David could have a career in cartography if he ever tires of painting) with black pointers indicating the direction of view. The page number of the painting is inside the pointer.

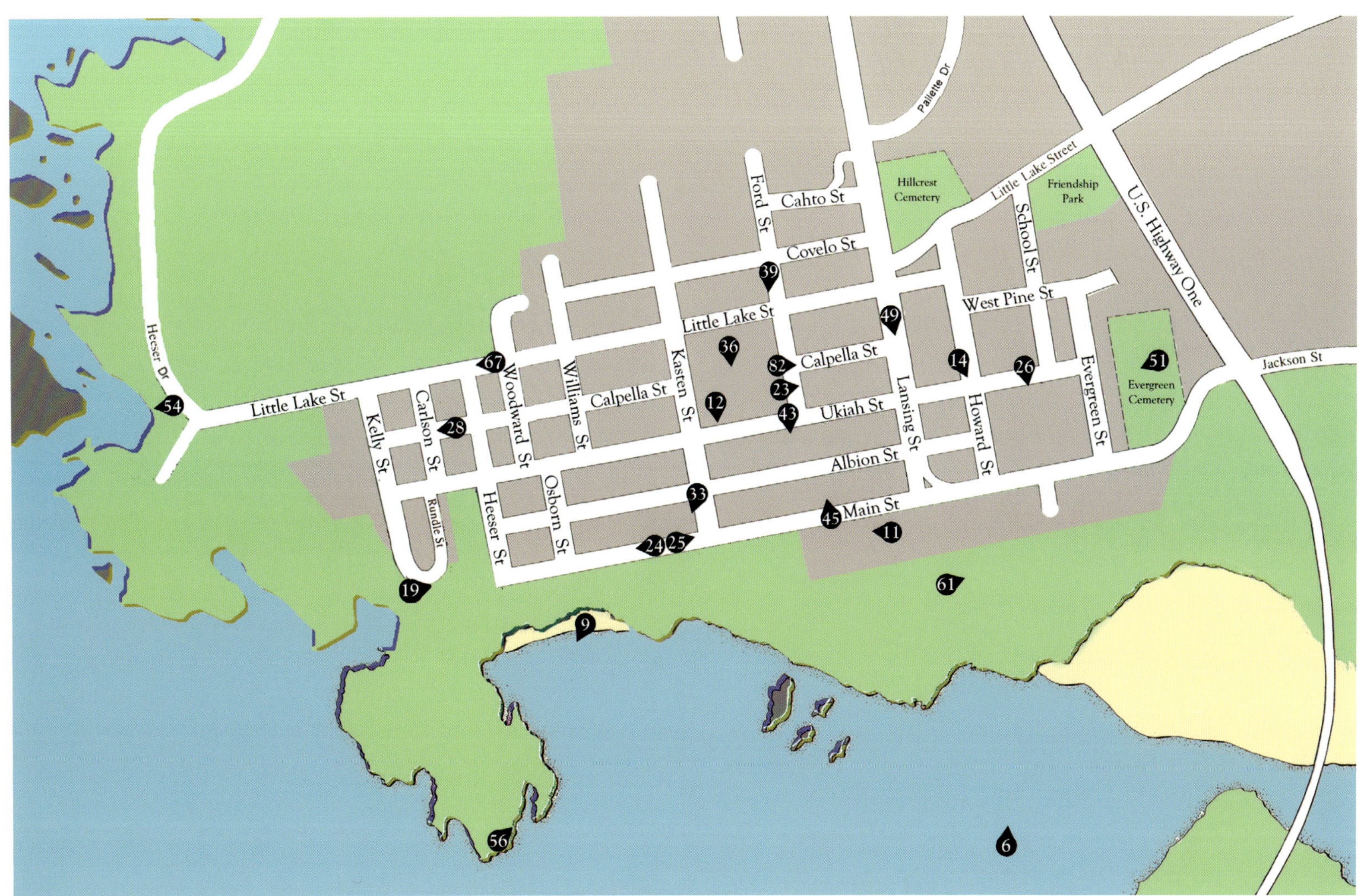

Mendocino City

When we first moved to Mendocino, it was to an oceanfront house south of town in a former quarry, whence the rocks needed to build the county airport had been scooped. The house was built right at the edge of the cliff, and there was a 50 foot drop down to the crashing surf. No fences; it would have spoiled the view. This was a challenging place to move with three under-10 children, a nervous mother-in-law, and a dog that may have had fewer neurons than a doorstop. On the first day, my wife, the girls, and I crawled on our bellies to the very edge of the cliff and peered over. "There," she said, "Now you've done it. Never do it again." They didn't. And we have three middle-aged daughters, with generally happy memories of their ten years here.

The dog, Samwise, a bearded collie, caused much concern as he raced along the cliff with wild abandon. But his only scary adventure came late one night when we called him in at bedtime. The poor creature was lying on his belly on the deck, whimpering, seemingly unable to move. When he made pitiful efforts to sit up, and could not, we phoned the vet's home number, and got him out of bed at midnight. He advised us to slide a blanket gently under the dog, bundle him up, and we'd meet at the clinic in half an hour. We tried ... which is when we discovered that the dog's ID and rabies tags had gotten wedged between two boards in the deck, so he was unable to stand up. Thankfully, Dr. Detrick had a good sense of humor, and is probably still telling that story.

The vocational high school offered a course in house-building, open to adults. We, another couple, and a dozen students built a small home, and gained both the knowledge and the courage to do our own. With the help of a local C.P.A., a sculptor, and a lady shingler who worked topless, we built a fine little home near Brewery Gulch. We sold our oceanfront house on six acres (for a six-digit price beginning with a 'one'!) to the Mendocino Hotel owner, who was never able to get permits for the restaurant he wanted on that spot. He, in turn, sold it to folks who quadrupled its size and gated the driveway. We haven't been invited to stop by for tea, but we've peered at it by bashing through the bushes from the adjoining cemetery, and are told it now has a *seven*-figure price (possibly still starting with a 'one').

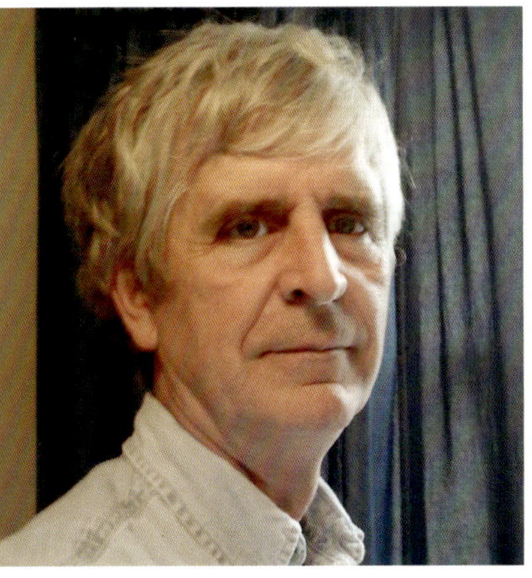

David Gregory is the eldest of fourteen siblings who were raised on the flat lands of central Illinois. He first visited Mendocino in 1976 and knew at once he wanted to live on that spectacular coast some day. In 1987 he moved to Mendocino to help promote the first edition of this book and remained for many years. Returning to Mendocino often, he enjoys hiking the headlands and wandering through the town in search of new subjects to paint. He now lives in Peoria, Illinois with his wife Renée and four children in various stages of flying out of and back into the nest. David studied painting, printmaking, and architecture at the University of Illinois. Since then, he has created over three thousand paintings and hundreds of etchings. He is a signature member of the Hawaii Watercolor Society and has received several awards in HWS shows. You can see more of his artwork at davidgregoryart.com.

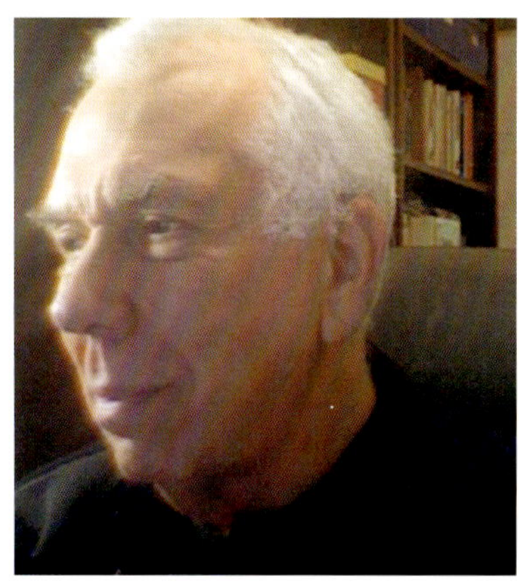

John Bear, his wife Marina and their three daughters moved to Mendocino in 1974, where they remained for ten years, writing books, starting and running the Flying Bear Candy Store in Fort Bragg and an ice cream parlor in Mendocino. After many years in the Bay Area, the lure of the coast was so strong, they returned, impractically, irrationally, but happily in 2010 for a year and a half—but as this book goes to press, they are making plans to divide their time between pieds-a-terre in Berkeley and Portland, Oregon, where their daughters now live. John is the author of more than thirty books with major publishers (education, computers, cooking, effective complaining), earned a Ph.D. at Michigan State University, in a weak moment was a contestant on Jeopardy, and believes he is the only person ever to be a consultant to the FBI and the Grateful Dead, albeit not simultaneously.

In physics, the Heisenberg Uncertainty Principle says it is impossible to measure tiny particles with accuracy because the very act of measuring them changes the size or behavior of what you are measuring. There is a kind of Heisenberg principle operating in Mendocino as well. The more successful we are in promoting growth, the more we change the very things that bring people to the region in the first place.

It is wonderful to have enough people, residents and visitors, to be able to support good restaurants, theater groups, a choice of health care professionals, good schools, satisfactory roads, and so forth. Too few and you don't have these things. But too many and lines grow longer, the classrooms are overcrowded, the roads clogged, the parking spaces harder to find, the water supply depleted, and the social services overburdened.

There is a precarious middle position between feast and famine, and it is nearly impossible to get people to agree on just what it is. Expand the airport? Limit new commercial construction? Build a convention center? Restrict the number of bed and breakfast conversions? Build a casino? (rumored since an Indian tribe bought 60 oceanfront acres from a bankrupt developer). These are some of the issues coastal people continue to wrestle with.

It has been twenty-five years since the first edition of this book. If we wait another twenty-five years to do a third edition, what might we expect to say (and paint)?

The Mendocino coast (or, as publisher Jim Tarbell calls it, the Fort Bragg Trade Area) has been evolving in a relatively healthy way. Unlike many other towns, this area keeps reinventing itself in progressive ways, not simply decaying and degrading. A major concern of thoughtful committed locals is to design a new and stable purpose for the area: one not based on timber, fishing, tourism, or cannabis. Education, research and development, and elder care have all been pipe-dreamed.

Mendocino as a charming tourist-oriented theme park, or a progressive, economically stable town of the future? The third edition of this book, hopefully sooner than 2036, may tell all. Thanks for joining us.

Book Ordering Information

Additional copies of this very book can be purchased directly from David (contact information to the right), or from Cypress House (www.cypresshouse.com).

The 1986 *Mendocino* book, long out of print, can sometimes be found used at Gallery Bookshop in Mendocino (www.gallerybookshop.com), or online at bookfinder.com, typically in the $50 – $70 range.

Some of John's other books (some with co-authors; all but the first two Ten Speed Press/Random House):

- *Not Your Mother's Cookbook: unusual recipes for the adventurous cook,* SLG Books, www.slgbooks.com
- *Degree Mills: the billion dollar industry that has sold a million fake diplomas* (www.PrometheusBooks.com)
- *How to Repair Food*
- *Morning Food*
- *Bears Guide to Earning Degrees by Distance Learning*
- *Send This Jerk the Bedbug Letter: how corporations, politicians and the media deal with consumer complaints*
- The #1 New York Times Bestseller

David Gregory Print Ordering Information

In case you were wondering, many of the paintings in this book can be purchased as Giclée prints. A Giclée is the finest art reproduction available. Pronounced zheek-lay, this process prints the work of art on watercolor paper or canvas with archival pigments, producing excellent color match and sharp detail, recreating the feel of the original work of art. Archival pigments are considered to be lightfast for 125 years.

These reproductions are printed on acid-free watercolor paper or acid-free 100% cotton canvas, the same surfaces David paints on.

Contact David by email at gregoryart@hotmail.com for size, price, and ordering information.

You can see additional works of art by David on his website: www.davidgregoryart.com